E IS FOR EXCEPTIONAL

THE NEW SCIENCE OF SUCCESS

ROB YEUNG

PAN BOOKS

First published 2010 by Macmillan as *The Extra One Per Cent*

This edition published 2012 by Pan Books
an imprint of Pan Macmillan, a division of Macmillan Publishers Limited
Pan Macmillan, 20 New Wharf Road, London N1 9RR
Basingstoke and Oxford
Associated companies throughout the world
www.panmacmillan.com

ISBN 978-1-4472-0998-0

1 3 5 7 9 8 6 4 2

A CIP catalogue record for this book is available from the British Library.

Printed and bound by CPI Group (UK) Ltd, Croydon, CR0 4YY

Visit www.panmacmillan.com to read more about all our books
and to buy them. You will also find features, author interviews and
news of any author events, and you can sign up for e-newsletters
so that you're always first to hear about our new releases.

CONTENTS

Acknowledgements

To my parents for allowing me to find my own path in life. To Steve and Byron for keeping me grounded.

To my many client organisations for inviting me to investigate what it takes to be a high achiever. To the many, many people who gave their time to be interviewed – especially the ones who didn't make it into the book because I didn't have enough space to include them!

To Liz Gough for her enthusiastic support and for allowing me to bring my work to a wider audience. To Becky Mallery for her help with research and Bonnie Chiang for her shrewd yet always encouraging comments.

INTRODUCTION

WHAT HELPS CERTAIN PEOPLE to become successful? What helps one person to soar and lift themselves from mediocrity, to become an exceptional leader, doctor, parent, entrepreneur, pop star, actor, teacher, or anything else?

To answer the question, let's think for a moment about the successful people you know and what makes them so accomplished. Consider your circle of friends, family, and acquaintances and single out the top handful of people you know. Now ask them about their secrets of success. Try it. Ask: 'In your opinion, what do you think you do that makes you so successful?'

They'll talk about the need for hard work, grit and determination, a need to stay focused even when things go wrong. But they may add that they must be willing to change course, be adaptable, or even quit when something isn't working.

They may talk about vision, confidence, passion, creativity, taking risks, and the need to trust their instincts at times. Dig a little deeper and they'll mention the importance of surrounding themselves with good people. They may even acknowledge an element of luck – of being in the right time and place too.

But interview enough brilliantly successful people and you'll discover that they all start to sound the same. They end up covering the same ground, making nearly identical assertions.

Read a business biography or hear any celebrity speak and they make the same generalisations too. Business moguls Richard Branson and Bill Gates sound remarkably like celebrities such as Madonna or Tom Cruise and even sporting luminaries such as Tiger Woods and Venus Williams.

In a way, they are all correct. They have the right ideas. But so, too, do many people who aren't very accomplished. I'm sure you know people who *think* they are visionary, creative, determined, adaptable, and all that. But they don't get the same results as the people they'd like to emulate. Because superstar performers can rarely articulate what they do in enough detail to help other people follow in their footsteps. So here's the question: how do we go about figuring out what *really* makes certain people so successful?

Defining success

Let's turn the focus on you for a moment. How successful would you say you are on a scale of 1 to 10? This book is about the science of success, on how academics and consultants have tried to identify what helps some people to succeed and reach the top end of the scale. In this book I shall share stories and scientific studies about exceptional people with the aim of understanding what they do differently that helps them to succeed. But this will also help you to understand how researchers go about investigating success. So bear with me for now and give yourself a number.

Most people give themselves a score of between 5 and 8. Hardly anyone ever says they're a 10 or even a 9 – that implies they've achieved everything there is to strive for in life. Plus it smacks of more than a little arrogance, right?

Very few people give themselves scores of 1 or 2 and you don't get many scores of 3 or 4 either. And when people do give themselves lower scores, they often say that they've gone through a rough patch but are on their way back up again.

Of course you may be thinking that it's an unfair question. You may rightly reason that the answer depends on the definition of success we're using, on the criteria we employ to measure accomplishment. You probably think of success as a combination of factors, including how much you earn, how much you enjoy your work, the extent to which you have loving relationships in your life, how much sex you get, the pleasure you get from time with friends, how healthy you are, how much leisure time you enjoy, and so on. If we take all of those factors into consideration then our scale of 1 to 10 looks terribly crude.

Sometimes simplicity helps us to make a point though. So, just as many researchers like to do, let me temporarily do away with all of those complex factors and look only at a narrow financial definition of success, at how much a person earns. Of course, I'm not saying that a rich investment banker is a better person than, say, a nurse. And I will come back to a fuller, more rounded definition of success. But for now, let's say that I don't care how much people enjoy their job or the extent to which they're good parents or anything else. All I care about is how much cash they take home.

What makes people exceptional?

Let me introduce you to William Chalk and Jasper Ahlquist, two men who score at opposite ends of the scale. They are both key account managers working for a European information technology company. 'Key account manager' is the in-vogue job title in lots of organisations, but essentially they are salespeople. They take the company's computer products and computer-related services and sell them to corporate clients.

I can say that Chalk and Ahlquist score at opposite ends of the scale because that's where their employer puts them. Last year, one of these men was in the top 10 per cent of the sales force, by virtue of selling more hardware, software and services than 90 per cent of the other key account managers. The other man was in the bottom 10 per cent of the sales team, unfortunately being outsold by 9 in 10 of his colleagues.

They have both been working for the firm for over four years. Not every year has been equally good or bad for them. However, year after year, one of them was always in the top 40 per cent of the sales team; the other was never out of the bottom 50 per cent.

Last year, one of them earned £482,520 in salary and bonuses, putting him in the top 10 per cent of the company. The other earned £107,950, putting him in the bottom 10 per cent.

So who was the high achiever? Was it Chalk or Ahlquist?

Actually, the answer to 'Who?' isn't really the interesting bit. To me, the interesting answer is to the question 'Why?'

Both men have degrees from good universities and track records of career progression. Both passed a gruelling selection process that involved multiple rounds of interviews with senior managers from across the organisation. Both are well liked too. But one is vibrantly more successful than the other.

Harnessing the winning formula

'Why are some people so much more successful than others?' was the question that I was asked to answer by Margaret Taylor, the head of human resources at the technology firm who had hired Chalk and Ahlquist. She explained that the technology sector was booming. Demand was high. The company was growing explosively. But fast as the business was expanding, some of their competitors were growing even more quickly. A major problem, a real constraint to their growth, was hiring enough good key account managers to keep up with demand.

Taylor admitted that the business had a patchy record when it came to hiring great salespeople. Sometimes they had hired new faces, occasionally announcing with pride that they had poached a top salesperson from a rival, only for those alleged stars to crash and burn.

The company was investing significant time and money in training their fresh recruits, but it typically took new salespeople over a year to get to grips with the company's specific products and ways of working. So it was generally only after 12 to 18 months that the company could figure out who was a hit and who was a dud.

Of course, Taylor knew *who* their top salespeople were – she just didn't know *why* they were special. She couldn't figure out how to replicate the magic in future recruits. Despite a number of conflicting theories running amongst the senior managers as to what made for a high-performing salesperson, she couldn't say with certainty what made certain sales superstars better than the rest.

Taylor and her colleagues had already tried interviewing the high performers and also-rans. The result? All of the interviewees had talked about more or less the same traits, the same skills. Even wildly successful people don't *really* know how they do it.

So she enlisted my help. She hired me to do some detective work, to interview the salespeople in depth to identify what set the high performers apart from the rest. What differentiated the top 10 per cent of their salespeople from the merely adequate or the poor ones? If only they could figure out the formula that made for a top salesperson, the company could recruit a truly exceptional sales force.

The psychology of literal high-fliers

This wasn't the first time I'd done this kind of project. And I'm not the only psychologist ever to look at the reasons why certain people succeed while others fail. No, modern psychologists are grateful to Colonel John C. Flanagan.

Let's travel back in time to the Second World War. It's 1941. Most of Europe as well as countries including Japan and China had already been at war for several years. The United States of America had yet to join the war, but was making preparations for its likely participation. The United States Army Air Forces (USAAF) was created on 20 June, bringing together a number of separate air units and unifying them under a single command.

Less than six months later, the Japanese navy launched their strike on Pearl Harbor on 7 December; 3,684 American personnel died. Hundreds of ships and aircraft were sunk, damaged, or utterly destroyed. The USA was abruptly dragged into the Second World War.

The USAAF was immediately ordered to ramp up its numbers of pilots not by hundreds, or thousands, but by tens of thousands. More men were being shot out of the air than were being trained. But training pilots to fly planes under combat conditions couldn't be done overnight. And not every trainee recruited into flight school made it. Thousands of cadets were killed during training accidents every year while thousands more were dropped for not being good enough.

You can imagine that the decision to drop a trainee from flight school wasn't taken lightly. Being told that you weren't good enough to become a pilot at a time when your nation was at war was emotionally scarring. Plus it was financially expensive to recruit trainees only to kick them out.

The expert tutors and check pilots who made the decisions were required to write up explanations as to why they had rejected cadets from the programme. They gave reasons such as 'unsuitable temperament', 'poor judgement', 'insufficient progress', or even 'lack of inherent flying ability'.

But what did such phrases mean? No one knew exactly. Certainly, the explanations weren't good enough to avoid recruiting the wrong kind of candidates. Thousands of recruits were being thrown out for unclear reasons, over and over again. Even worse, thousands more young cadets continued to be killed in training accidents every year.

The USAAF realised that even experienced instructors and check pilots were making unhelpful generalisations when evaluating trainees. Grasping the problem, the USAAF set up a task force to investigate in depth why certain trainee pilots made the grade while others fell short. Civilian psychologist John C. Flanagan was enlisted to head the research.

Making better decisions

Flanagan was faced with an enormous task, a huge responsibility, which quickly exploded into a monumental one. The USAAF was recruiting breathtaking numbers of people to fight the war. On 31 December 1941, the USAAF had 354,161 personnel flying and fixing over 12,000 planes. Only two years later, the USAAF had swelled to 2,373,882 servicemen and women looking after 64,000 planes.

Flanagan came to a seismic conclusion: most people – whether the trainee pilots themselves or their highly experienced instructors – were almost useless at explaining what contributed to even phenomenal success or dreadful failure. In a report of his findings, he wrote: 'Too often, statements regarding job requirements are merely lists of all the desirable traits of human beings. These are practically no help in selecting, classifying, or training individuals for specific jobs.'[1]

So he changed tactic. He stopped asking for general opinions as to why missions typically failed or succeeded. Instead, he urged pilots to talk about specific episodes of either triumph or failure in forensic detail, with a particular focus on what they did, what they said and what they were thinking at the time.

Over several years, Flanagan recruited a team of over 150 psychologists and more than 1,000 assistants. Together, they helped him to interview tens of thousands of personnel, asking them to describe specific instances in which they had succeeded or failed. In doing so, he made a tangible contribution to the war effort. His seminal research enabled the USAAF to make better recruitment decisions, turning away more candidates who were unlikely to make it through pilot training or perhaps even more likely to kill themselves in the process. Flanagan was later awarded the Legion of Merit for the outstanding contribution that he and his team made towards winning the war.

Talking about specific examples

Flanagan and his colleagues conceived and refined the interviewing method known as the critical incident technique (CIT),[2] a method that psychologists continue to use today. His technique allows us to unpack what helps to differentiate successful hotshots from the crowd. It was this method that I used to interview Margaret Taylor's salespeople, the key account managers such as Chalk and Ahlquist.

Rather than asking for general opinions as to *why* people think they succeed or fail, the idea is to solicit detailed descriptions of *what* they did in the past. Rather than asking, 'What do you do?' or 'What do you *think* you do?', the emphasis becomes 'What *did* you do?'

The goal is to hear about specific episodes of either success or failure in almost excruciating detail in order to understand what people did, the options they considered, and the moment-by-moment actions they took. To give you an idea of the technique in action, here's the introductory spiel I used at the start of each interview with Taylor's computer salespeople. Over the years I've repeated many, many similar introductions:

'We're currently doing a study of what constitutes sales success in the key account manager role so we can improve training programmes and make smarter hiring decisions in the future. We believe you are especially well qualified to tell us about successful selling.

'I'd most like to hear you talk about specific examples of situations in which you made a sale. Rather than talk about your opinions or how you generally go about selling to clients, I'd like to hear about particular instances that you can talk through in depth. Don't worry if you can't remember all of the details, but I would ideally like to get at a lot of the detail if we can – what the client said or did, what you said or did next, how the client responded, what happened next, and so on.

'Take a few moments to think about a specific instance where you were outstandingly effective in making a sale to a client. Can you talk me through it, please?'

As you've no doubt noticed, my introduction is a little repetitive. I talk about 'specific examples', 'particular instances', and 'a specific instance'. But the key to the critical incident technique is to get as full a description as possible. The idea is to get a retelling that almost reads like a moment-by-moment transcript of who said what, who did what, how, and when. Detail is good. Generalisations and opinions are bad, remember.

The fuller and more detailed their descriptions, the more likely they are to have been remembered correctly. When an interviewee says, 'I persuaded the client to take a small consignment,' I then unleash a torrent of further questions: 'What did you say to persuade the client?' and then 'How did the client respond?' followed by 'What did you do next?' and 'What happened next?', and so on.

If it looks like a lot of questions, you're right. It is. It's more like a police interrogation than a traditional interview, because I'm constantly trying to keep each interviewee focused on retelling one single situation rather than risk them slipping into overly broad opinions about what they generally do. I want to soak up the details of every little action they took, the thoughts they had, and ultimately the results they achieved.

Themes and patterns

Once I'd interviewed enough people at the technology firm, I analysed the stories to understand the seemingly trivial differences in behaviour that distinguished high achievers from their less prosperous counterparts. Top key account managers tended to spend more time engaging in social chit-chat and building rapport before getting down to business, for example. They sent fewer emails and made more phone calls. They also tried to influence clients in both direct and indirect methods – not only meeting with clients but also spending considerable time with people who could put in a good word with clients too.

By analysing the differences between what high- and low-achieving salespeople talked about, I built a list of the behaviours that distinguished between exceptional and merely average performance. To use the corporate jargon, I created a set of 'competencies' or a 'competency framework'.

Working out precisely which behaviours separate the best people from the rest allows organisations to hire the right kinds of people and reject the wrong ones. An organisation can think about how to train people, how to develop the next generation of exceptional leaders, doctors, technicians, customer service agents, or whatever else it needs. But competency frameworks aren't just for big businesses. Individuals benefit too – most organisations publish their competencies and encourage employees to read about the kind of behaviours that are expected of them. Achievement-oriented people can think about how to improve themselves, make plans, and measure their progress as they go.

Matters we can control

Here's a couple of seemingly random facts for you, which may seem like a bit of a tangent. Read on for now and I'll explain shortly.

Did you know that taller people tend to earn more money? Researcher Timothy Judge at the University of Florida looked at earnings and height data for 8,590 men and women in both the UK and US. Taking differences in gender, age, and weight into consideration, he found that taller people tend to earn more money. He estimated that each extra inch in height tended to earn a person more than an extra $700 a year.[3]

In a separate study, Norwegian scientists Petter Kristensen and Tor Bjerkedal found that first-born children tend to have higher intelligence scores than second-born children, who in turn tend to have higher intelligence scores than third-born children.[4]

All around the world, there are many similar studies looking at the causes of success, what causes some people to be more intelligent, to earn more, to thrive. Other studies show that our chances of prosperity are also affected by our parents' level of education[5] and the upbringing we had as children.[6] But how can we apply such lessons?

Answer: we can't.

We can't easily alter our height (although it does suggest a reason why high heels are so popular and a certain short male Hollywood star is alleged to wear lifts in his shoes). We can't change the circumstances of our birth. We can't go back and tamper with our parents, our background, our culture, or where we come from. Such research doesn't help us to improve our lives, to become more prosperous ourselves.

The competency movement is different. Rather than looking into the unchangeable characteristics of people that lead to success, it focuses on the behaviours that lead to success. That's why I'm a fan. Because competency research focuses on *what people do*, and *what they think and say*, rather than what they are. It looks at what we can all learn to do rather than the innate differences in people that we can do nothing about. Ultimately, competency research is wonderfully inspiring because it shows us what we can do; it points to what we can choose to change about ourselves if we want to develop the potential we have.

A rich picture of success

So far I've focused almost exclusively on money as a measure of success. Of course, true prosperity isn't only about currency though. Yes, it helps to have a bit of cash in life and I'll certainly be talking about the behaviours that help people to earn more. However, people can be financially rich while feeling lonely because they have too few friends. They can hate their work and wish they had taken another path. Or struggle with internal demons that prevent them from enjoying their material wealth. A big pay cheque and the corner office do not guarantee happiness.

Success is not only about salary, but also about career satisfaction, having an abundance of affirming relationships, being a good parent, leaving a positive legacy behind, being in good health and feeling fulfilled, and even having fun. It can mean feeling challenged, alive, and able to sleep at night, rather than bored, stressed, or tormented. In this book I shall look at all of these factors and incorporate them into the fullest definition of success possible. What do certain individuals do, say or think that allows them to reach to dizzying heights while others stay mired in mere adequacy?

Over the years, I've run interviews with hundreds and hundreds of employees and managers in all sorts of roles in organisations spanning law firms, government departments, high street banks and insurance businesses, advertising agencies, management consultancies, charities, airlines, and even a pet products company. Irrespective of where I've conducted the research – working with a national business or a global one, a public sector organisation or a private sector business, an organisation selling intangible services or one that manufactures physical goods – the same kinds of behaviours crop up again and again.

Even across disciplines, there are unifying themes as to what hotshot individuals do, how they behave, even how they think and make decisions. And it's these themes that I shall explore in this book, the broad attitudes and behaviours that are associated with high performance across most fields and disciplines. Come with me as I focus on what you *can* change, what you *can* influence, what you can *do* to make the best of yourself and achieve your potential.

The science and stories of success

The inventor Thomas Edison famously quipped that genius was 99 per cent perspiration and only 1 per cent inspiration. Every successful person I've ever interviewed talked about the perspiration they put in. Successful people work hard. But people who work hard don't always succeed. Because there's a big difference between working long, hard hours and working on the *right* things. And that's what this book is about: the often subtle, yet crucial differences that separate the best from the rest.

As you can imagine, the study of success has attracted quite a few researchers over the years. Scientists all over the globe have looked at the behaviours and techniques that separate high-flying individuals from the rest. Without the backing of scientific evidence, we risk wandering into the realm of self-help quacks and fraudsters.[7] So throughout the book I shall also draw on world-class research to demonstrate what works and what doesn't.

I've also listened to many stories of success first-hand. So I shall share some of these narratives too. I've changed a few of the names of people I interviewed. Occasionally they revealed sensitive information. In other cases, large organisations decided that they didn't want to single people out for special treatment. By allowing one person to be mentioned as a high achiever, they feared that other colleagues who didn't get profiled may feel left out and not so special. Thankfully, many of the entrepreneurs I interviewed own their businesses and make their own rules. So I've been able to use real names and details more often than not.

I can't promise startling secrets that guarantee your success. However, I will use scientific evidence and swirl in stories of successful people to construct a picture of what separates exceptional people from the rest to help you achieve more in life.

The capabilities of exceptional people

Many consultants and academics like to use the term 'competencies' to describe the skills and behaviours of successful people. But I don't like the word. Who only wants to be *competent*? Surely we want to be extraordinary, outstanding, exceptional?

I prefer to describe the different categories of behaviours as 'capabilities', because these are skills that we are all capable of. So, broadly speaking, what does distinguish exceptional people from everybody else? In today's ever more hectic, multicultural, technologically advanced world, eight broad capabilities seem to make the difference:

- **Awe.** Exceptional people aren't just born more creative – they fuel their imaginations by actively pursuing new experiences and consciously staying open-minded about, or 'in awe' of, new possibilities. Rather than assuming they know enough about their field or industry, they remain curious and realise that there is always more to learn and consider.

- **Cherishing.** We all have built-in abilities that allow us to sense how other people might be feeling, or what they might be thinking. But we need to make a conscious effort to use these skills – they don't always come automatically. High-performing individuals take the time to listen and understand other people's feelings and their perspectives because it helps them to smooth over any interpersonal differences and influence and persuade others.

- **Authenticity.** High performers in any field routinely say that they love what they do. Authenticity is the ability to discover our own motivations and our sometimes hidden strengths, and then to find both work and personal situations that allow us to feel fulfilled and 'alive'. People who feel passionate every day give themselves the best shot at achieving extraordinary results.

- **Centredness.** High achievers have the ability to remain focused and motivated even in the face of extreme adversity. They recover quickly from both personal disappointments and professional catastrophes. By dealing with even toxic emotions such as despair or anger, they restore their emotional equilibrium, which allows them to perform at their best.

- **Connecting.** High-fliers recognise the power that comes from working with others. They value and seek out collaborations, partnerships, teams, networks, and coalitions. Rather than trying to take on everything themselves, they reach out to diverse others, asking for help and building many, many mutually rewarding relationships.

- **Daring.** While many people shy away from failure, exceptional people are ready to chance failure time and again by taking calculated risks. High achievers realise that it's only through unfettered exploration, taking opportunities when they arise, and making the occasional mistake that they can truly push themselves and achieve outstanding results.

- **Citizenship.** Exceptional people with the skill of Citizenship think about the bigger picture of their work and lives. They consider the broader impact of what they do and how it affects everybody around them. They have integrity and behave ethically and responsibly. And, rather than thinking only in terms of months and quarters, they think in terms of years and decades – they take the long view.

- **Visioning.** This capability is about creating a balanced vision of the life that we crave to lead. While many people are talented and ambitious, exceptional individuals realise that their visions must encompass not only *what* they want to achieve but *who they want to be* on a day-to-day basis. Because success – not just *being* successful but *feeling* successful and fulfilled – comes from working towards future goals while at the same time savouring day-to-day events.

I shall use scientific evidence to argue that these capabilities already distinguish many iconic people from their less stellar counterparts. And, if anything, I believe that these will become even more indispensable in the near future as global competition and the pace of change continue to increase.

A book to read, a plan to follow

Reading about virtuoso individuals, the skills they possess and the actions they take is no doubt stirring and uplifting. By all means read this book if you wish simply to be entertained.

If you wish to apply the lessons contained within this book, you will have to *use* the book. Based on the research and knowledge we have available, I provide practical tools to help you achieve your goals – whether that's to become a thriving entrepreneur, manager, parent, fund-raiser, whatever. I include 'Over to you' boxes, which are quick opportunities for you to reflect on what you've read or try something that will take no more than a minute.

'Become your best' boxes offer deeper exercises or techniques to try. These take more time, but could help you to become more effective, make better decisions, and move closer towards your goals. Taking the book as a whole, you will find sensible, hype-free advice for achieving your potential in either your life or the lives of those around you.

Shall we get started?

ONE

AWE

'Imagination is more important than knowledge.'

Albert Einstein

ASK EXCEPTIONAL PEOPLE ABOUT their journey to the top and they are usually the first to stress how hard they worked to get there. When I've interviewed stars in disciplines ranging from business and philanthropy to medicine and entertainment, they talk about the determination it took, the often long hours and doggedness with which they worked. High achievers are driven, ambitious, and resolute in the pursuit of their goals. So being focused is good, right?

Well, depends. Those traits could easily become the very opposite of what it takes to succeed too. Because there's only a fine line that separates being focused from being narrow-minded.

Allowing for opportunities

Imagine you're watching some video footage of six people – two teams of three – playing basketball. The video clip only lasts 75 seconds so you don't have to concentrate for long. One of the teams is wearing white T-shirts and the other is dressed in black T-shirts. 45 seconds into the game, a person wearing a black gorilla suit strolls into the middle of the screen, pounds its chest, and walks off screen. The gorilla is visible on screen for five seconds. You'd notice, right?

Maybe not.

Harvard University psychologists Daniel Simons and Christopher Chabris tempted undergraduate students into watching the video clip I just described in exchange for either a candy bar or a small payment. The researchers gave the students a task: to count the number of times the ball was passed between members of the team in white. Immediately after watching the film, the students were told to write down how many passes they'd counted. The researchers then asked,

'Did you see anyone else besides the six players appear on the video?' and 'Did you see a gorilla walk across the screen?'

More than half of the participants were puzzled. What gorilla? They hadn't seen any gorilla.[8]

Well how about if we offered to pay people cash as an incentive for noticing what was going on around them? In a similar experiment to the one conducted by the Harvard team, Richard Wiseman, a University of Hertfordshire professor of psychology, asked a group of volunteers to flip through a newspaper. Their task? Simply to count the number of photographs they came across.[9]

Straightforward enough. After several pages, there was a half-page advert with the words: 'Stop counting. There are 43 photographs in this newspaper.' But most people kept on turning the pages, too engrossed in counting the photos to see the answer.

A few pages later, another bigger advert proclaimed: 'Stop counting. Tell the experimenter you've seen this and win £150.' Again, most people didn't notice it. Oblivious to the cash prize, they diligently carried on with the task despite the answer being literally spelt out in black and white. Only a handful of people spotted the adverts, usually laughing and asking to claim their winnings.

Do you have the time to read this?

I was once invited to run a day-long workshop for a group of managers to discuss fresh product ideas that would allow them to beat their competition. To highlight how narrowly our minds can sometimes work, I began by asking the audience if they had the time for me to tell them a story.

A few of them checked their watches and gave me the go-ahead. I then asked them to tell me what time it was. Most of the managers chuckled. They didn't know. Despite having just looked at their watches, they had to look again. The first time they looked at their watches, they weren't looking to tell the time. They were looking to see if they had enough time to listen to a story before the end of the session.

Harvard psychology professor Ellen Langer has been using the same test on her college students for years. At some point during each semester, she asks each fresh class of students if they have the time to allow her to tell them a story. Every time, she finds that they have to look twice to be able to say what time it is. Based on her observations, she concludes: 'What we have learned to look for in a situation determines mostly what we see.'[10]

All three of these examples highlight a phenomenon that psychologists call 'inattentional blindness'. When we look for one thing, we may fail to notice others. Focusing our attention too intently on any particular goal or direction may blind us to other opportunities.[11]

Our culture celebrates the cult of working hard and being focused. We're told that focusing intently on a goal until its completion is a good thing. But the real world doesn't come in neat little packages.

If we bury ourselves in a task at work – say sorting through our expenses or writing agendas for meetings – we may not consider whether we could do away with the task entirely. Charge around trying to sell a product to customers and we may miss the fact that the product is no longer right for their needs and we need to fashion a better one. Or if we go to a party looking to meet the love of our life, we may be closed off to meeting people who could become close friends or people who could help us in our careers, or in other ways.

Get too fixed on a specific goal and we may not spot those other openings. Unless we're careful, too much focus could easily blinker us to other ideas and opportunities, making our minds less fertile and less creative.

OVER TO YOU

Of course you have goals in life. But avoid being too focused on the daily tasks you want to complete such as clearing your inbox, getting those reports done, getting to work, and getting the household chores done. Although routines help us to get tasks done more quickly, it's easy for us all to get stuck in ruts.[12] In a quest for efficiency, our routines may stop us from trying out new ways of doing things and being more creative.

It's often the random events – the seeming disruptions to our daily patterns – that can stimulate creativity. Thinking about your schedule for tomorrow, what one small change could you introduce into your day? What could you do differently?

Forgetting to be creative

Let me introduce you to Alexander Michl. He's worked in creative industries his entire adult life. Starting out as a graphic designer, he progressed to being a creative director for advertising agencies in Europe and North America, establishing a reputation for innovative campaigns with technology brands such as Toshiba, Intel, and Compaq. He also currently nurtures the next generation of creative minds by teaching on a design Master of Arts programme at Central Saint Martins in London, the institution that produced designers Terence Conran and Stella McCartney.

Yet he tells me that even people who have creative job titles can forget to be creative. A few years ago, he was signed up as art director at one of the largest picture supply companies in the world.

The company had for years made its money from selling high-quality images to advertising companies for use in their campaigns. So the creative department's ongoing remit was to generate ever more high-quality images.

'The whole creative team was going out to art exhibitions and being on top of fashion and style. Yet they were oblivious to what was going on in the world of technology,' Michl tells me.

Two developments blindsided the team. One, the cost of digital photographic equipment plummeted almost as quickly as its quality was going up, allowing even amateurs to take nearly professional-quality photos. Two, amateurs woke up to the fact that they could showcase their images on the Internet for people all over the world at almost no cost.

The creative team that Michl joined continued doing what it had always done. It was a nearly fatal mistake.

A year later, online companies began selling high-quality photos taken by amateurs and hobbyists for as little as a few dollars. Michl's employer was still charging hundreds or even thousands of dollars for their shots. True, the quality wasn't quite as good, but the price differential was too huge for buyers to ignore. Almost overnight, the share price of the media supply company halved. And all because the creative team had been so intently focused on the task they thought they needed to do that they didn't spot the opportunities elsewhere.

Cultivating conscious creativity

Some people confuse creativity with artistry, believing that creativity is optional, perhaps not even necessary for what they do. But let me define creativity as the act of coming up with ideas that allow us to make a difference to our lives and those of the people around us. We all need it. Creativity allows engineers to build new machines, office workers to devise quicker ways of working, and parents to find new ways of entertaining the kids.

Organisations want to innovate too, to conjure up new products and services to serve their customers in ways that will inspire their loyalty and devotion. At the very least, businesses such as Alexander Michl's employer need to spot threats and opportunities on the horizon before it's too late.

We can gain a real edge by inventing fresh answers to problems that stump others. And the good news is that we can *learn* to become more creative. Far from being a mysterious process, researchers increasingly believe that creativity can be taught. Robert Sternberg, a professor at Tufts University and one of the world's foremost investigators into creativity, argues that we can all become more imaginative. Based on over three decades of research, he concludes: 'Our fundamental premise is that creativity is in large part a decision that anyone can make but that few people actually do make.'[13]

So it's a myth that creativity is a rarefied gift imparted only to certain people. Original thinking instead appears to come about as the result of decisions and actions that anyone can choose to take. Sure, some people may still be born with more of a resourceful knack than others. But Sternberg is saying that radical ideas come about as much through conscious effort and hard work as natural talent. He's quite emphatic on this point, going on to say: 'To be creative one must first *decide* to generate new ideas...The skill is not enough: one first needs to make the decision to use the skill.'

Great – we can all become more deliberately creative if we take the decision to do so. The question is: how?

Igniting our capability for Awe

We know from the work of scientists such as Robert Sternberg that creativity is the end result of the conscious decisions we make rather than an esoteric gift that only certain people are born with. Creativity comes about as the result of activity. Individuals who make time to question, speculate and learn about the world tend to be more creative. They have the capability of Awe.

Of course we're all curious about the world, you may say. However, the critical bit here is making space in our schedules for such exploration. Awe is the ability to *make time* for curiosity, inquisitiveness, and wonderment about the world. How much time do most of us allow ourselves to express that curiosity? After all, it takes time to daydream and wonder 'What if?' and 'How could we?'

Researchers have established that people with a greater need for closure, a desire to reach a quick answer – any answer – tend to be less creative in group discussions.[14] The more people want to get to an end result of some sort, the less they seem able to make radical departures. So sometimes we should read, engage, and learn about the world not because we need that learning to be applied to a specific problem we're currently facing, but for its own sake, because we're curious.

Some companies are famous for giving their people time to explore, think, and concoct. Technology and science company

3M prides itself on giving employees scope and freedom to imagine and invent. Famously, the company instituted a policy encouraging technical staff members to spend up to 15 per cent of their work time on projects of their own choosing, projects that weren't necessarily within their job remit. Their 15 per cent rule helped the company to birth some of 3M's most famous products, including Post-it Notes and Scotch Tape.

Online giant Google goes further by letting its engineers spend 20 per cent of their work time – a day a week – working on projects that they are passionate about. Products such as Google Mail and Google News came about as a result of employee tinkering and experimentation during their '20 per cent time'.

Sadly, the vast majority of companies don't place enough value on original thinking and innovation. Sure, they *say* that they want employees to be creative, to come up with fresh ideas, and innovate. But do they allocate time for their people to do it? Rarely.

It's up to us as individuals to carve out time for creative thinking – not because it will be good for our organisations, but because it will be good for us. If we are too focused on rushing from one task to the next, from achieving one goal to pursuing the next, we may fail to explore the ideas and opportunities around us.

My research shows that high achievers take an active decision to stop what they're doing occasionally to ask if there might be an entirely better way of doing it. And we can learn from them. We need to make time to absorb new ideas, to think, question, speculate, and ultimately produce new insights and breakthroughs.

People with a greater need for closure tend to be less radical than individuals who can hold back their instinct to settle quickly on an answer. So people who make the effort to generate several ideas are far more likely to come up with a startling solution than someone who settles for the first one they come across.

When you're faced with a predicament, how often do you tend to dive straight in? Spending a few more moments considering different options could save you time further down the line. Can you commit to giving it a go the next time you're faced with a problem?

Feeding the fires of creativity

Psychologists believe that the more knowledge, information, and concepts we have in our brains, the more likely we are to be creative. We don't necessarily know how the knowledge and ideas we've accumulated allow us to generate new ones. They just swirl around in our heads and blend together in some mysterious fashion.

I call it the Uncertain Idea Percolator. Imagine that our minds are like a coffee filter. We feed in ideas and knowledge – the coffee grains and hot water – but need to wait for them to drip, drip, drip through the filter of our unconsciousness. Just as we can't tell which coffee grain has produced which droplet of coffee, we can't know for certain what knowledge may have led to which new idea. But in the same way that more coffee grains means a richer brew, the more ideas and knowledge we shove in, the more ideas will percolate through.[15]

Intuitively makes sense, doesn't it? That the more time we spend on learning, thinking, and questioning, the more likely we will be to come up with new concepts, solutions, and answers to help us get ahead.

Richard Boyatzis, a professor at Case Western Reserve University in the United States, has spent over a decade looking at the behaviours linked to high attainment. In one study, he assessed the behaviours and subsequent performance of outstanding partners at a mammoth professional services and consulting firm.[16] He began by interviewing the outstanding partners and rating them on behaviours such as their level of planning, self-confidence, coaching, and leadership. He then monitored the performance of the partners over seven successive quarters, tracking not only how much money they brought into the business but also the profitability of the work. Despite looking at over 20 different skills, he found that only two were linked to both revenue generation and profitability over the nearly two-year period. Which two skills? They were called 'values learning' and 'facilitates learning'. In other words, learning led to financial success.

Making an effort to learn is especially important as we get older. As children we're expected to learn, but as adults we sometimes think we know enough. Problem is: knowledge and accepted wisdom change all of the time. Knowledge is rarely absolute. Scientists in fields ranging from physics and chemistry to biology and engineering are always learning new concepts and discovering that what they thought they knew was only part of the story or even entirely wrong.

Medicine is one constantly changing field. Until relatively recently, doctors typically prescribed antacid drugs for stomach ulcers, believing that they were caused by stress, spicy foods, and excess acid. In the 1980s, medical scientist Barry Marshall suggested that stomach ulcers were caused by bacteria and earned only scorn and derision from the medical community.

But in 2005, he was awarded a Nobel Prize for his discovery of the bacterium *Helicobacter pylori*. Stomach ulcers are now treated with antibiotics, not antacids.

In disciplines such as law and finance, the rules change constantly as governments lay down new legislation and do away with the old. And of course technology is moving faster too.

In all sorts of fields, the accepted wisdom does change from time to time. What's taken as fact is shown to be myth. Knowledge is superseded. New theories, concepts, and ideas spring up to replace even deep-rooted ones. Change happens.

Building the T-shaped mind

On the 27th floor of a pristine glass-fronted building in Dubai, I'm sitting in a small, messy office. Despite a clean desk policy within the building, Richard Groenewald can't bear to throw anything away. 'You never know when you might need it,' he tells me.

Groenewald is head of human resources for the MEA (Middle East and Africa) division of a global bank with close to 10,000 employees.

Human resources is traditionally seen as a back office, administrative function more interested in the paper shuffling of hiring and firing than customer or business needs. Groenewald, however, doesn't see himself as working in human resources.

'I am not an HR person. I am not even a banking person,' he says. 'My job is to read the social, political, demographic, and business trends that may affect the business. I have to predict the kind of people we will need running our business five to ten years out and think through how we recruit, select, develop, and retain them.'

Of course he reads about business and human resources as well as attending conferences about his discipline. But that's expected of him. He believes that keeping the bigger picture in mind is more critical and is what helps him to stand out from other human resources professionals in becoming an effective adviser.

On his monthly visits to corporate HQ in London, he goes to a book shop famous for its extensive range of magazines. He moves from section to section, gathering a stack of a dozen or more magazines to read. Apart from certain favourites, he tries to vary his selection as much as possible. 'As long as it's written in the English language and it's not pornographic, I am willing to try any magazine once,' he says.

His perennial favourites include *The Economist*, *Monocle*, *Wired*, the *New Yorker*, and *New Scientist*. But his office offers countless examples of other purchases: *Runner's World*, *Black Beauty*, *Woman & Home*, *Broadcast*, *Junior*, *Diva*, *Rolling Stone*, and even *Airliner World*.

By deliberately deciding to read widely outside of his field, Groenewald is a good example of what has been called the 'T-shaped mind', comprising not only deep knowledge in certain areas (the vertical pillar of the 'T') but also a breadth of information across many areas (the horizontal bar of the 'T').[17]

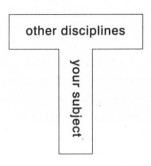

Time and again, researchers return to the conclusion that creativity comes about as the result of combining concepts that may have been previously unrelated. Game-changing products and innovative services often involve jamming previously unrelated notions together rather than simply trying to do something faster, better, or more cheaply.

Being inventive in your field is unlikely to come only from growing your knowledge about your particular subject or discipline, i.e. by increasing the length of the vertical pillar of your knowledge 'T'. The creative ideas are likely to come from mashing together disciplines such as politics, computer gaming, history, science, military strategy, and art. And that happens by broadening the horizontal bar of your knowledge 'T'.

We are faced with some big issues in the world – challenges such as pollution of the environment, terrorism, poverty, climate change, malnourishment, and water shortages. To deal with such issues, we are increasingly seeing teams coming together comprising scientists, economists, engineers, psychologists, medical researchers, politicians, and perhaps even celebrities to raise the profile of such work. In that kind of world, deep knowledge about only one discipline is a necessary – but insufficient – condition for truly creative thinking.

OVER TO YOU

Original thinking comes from having *both* deep knowledge about your field *and* broad knowledge about the world in general. Where are the gaps in your knowledge 'T'?

Learning isn't the same as education or mere reading though. Learning is about *experiencing* new topics in eclectic ways such as video presentations, online training programmes, interactive workshops, shadowing people, hands-on experience, and through meeting new people and engaging them in exploratory conversation or vigorous debate.

In terms of depth, what could you do to extend your knowledge of your field, discipline, or specialist area(s)? What two or three actions could you pledge to take in the coming months to develop your technical knowledge?

In terms of breadth, how could you expand your knowledge of ideas and advancements going on in the rest of the world? Think about particularly well-read or knowledgeable people you know. What do they do – in terms of reading, experiences, talking to people, travelling and living abroad, and so on – that you could incorporate into your life?

Travel, cultures, and creativity

I've been talking a lot about creativity. Ever wonder how researchers measure it?

Here's an example of one creativity test, called the Duncker candle problem.[18] You might want to try it if you haven't come across it before. Look at the picture below.

Imagine you're ushered into a room with a small table pushed against the wall. There are some objects on the table: a candle, a pack of matches, and a box of tacks. Your task is simple: you must figure out how to attach the candle to the wall so that the candle burns properly but does not drip wax on either the table or floor.

According to Karl Duncker, there's only one correct answer. I'll tell you what it is at the end of this section if you want to give it a go first.

Duncker's test is just one of the many tests that researchers use to examine the ways in which we can boost our creative ingenuity. For example, we know that travel broadens the mind, right? When we leave our home country, we get the opportunity to see different landscapes and architecture, sample exotic foods, interact with new people, perhaps wrap our lips around a few phrases of an unfamiliar language, and generally immerse ourselves in novel cultures. Rather than eating apples, oranges, and pears, we may be exposed to cherimoyas, biribas and jaboticabas in Latin America or langsats, durians, and mabolos in Asia.

We may learn that actions and gestures can be imbued with different meanings in different cultures too. For example, leaving food on your plate at a host's house is a sign of appreciation in cultures in Jordan and China, implying that the host has been generous and hospitable. In other countries, such as the UK or Indonesia, the same gesture may be seen as an insult, signalling disapproval about the quality of the food.[19]

Our intuition tells us that travel and exposure to new cultures must be good for creativity. Unfortunately, studies show that even extensive travel abroad does *not* necessarily enhance original thinking.

Researchers William Maddux from INSEAD business school and Adam Galinsky at Northwestern University asked 205 MBA students to report how much time they had spent both travelling and living in foreign countries before giving them the Duncker candle problem.[20] Only 54 per cent of the volunteers were able to solve the conundrum correctly (so don't feel bad if you can't work out the solution). However, looking into the backgrounds of the participants uncovered a revealing pattern. 60 per cent of people who had lived abroad were able to identify the correct solution, while only 48 per cent of people who had not lived abroad found the right answer. In addition, the longer people had lived abroad, the more likely they were to spot the answer. That makes sense, proving what we've known all along: that living abroad broadens the mind and enhances creativity.

The results didn't look so straightforward when it came to time spent travelling abroad though. Travelling abroad (i.e. visiting foreign countries but not moving there) did not improve the chances of finding the right answer. Even though some of the MBA students had travelled extensively around the world as part of their jobs, they didn't seem to have benefited creatively from it. That can't be right, can it?

Let's look at another study to shed light on this seemingly counter-intuitive finding.[21] Angela Leung at Singapore Management University and Chi-yue Chiu at the University of Illinois at Urbana-Champaign invited groups of American undergraduates to watch a 45-minute slide show before completing a test of creativity. Participants were randomly assigned to one of five groups. Four of the groups watched a multimedia slide presentation incorporating still images, background music, video clips, and movie trailers about a particular culture or cultures.

The first group watched a presentation devoted entirely to American culture while a second group watched a slide show focused only on Chinese culture. A third group watched a dual culture presentation of both American and Chinese images presented in alternate slides. A fourth group watched a slide show depicting elements of American–Chinese fusion, such as pictures of the McDonald's rice burger, images from the Shanghai Tang fashion line, and sequences from a Vanessa Mae music video. The fifth group was not shown a presentation and was directed only to complete the creativity test to provide the researchers with a baseline measure of creativity.

So which of the four presentations do you think pumped up creative ingenuity?

I should mention that the research team studied American undergraduates at a Midwestern American university. The first group watched the presentation dedicated solely to American culture, its architecture, scenery, home furnishings, clothing, cuisine, arts, and so on. Unsurprisingly, this first group was no more creative than the control group.

Perhaps more surprisingly, though, the second group that was exposed to 45 minutes of purely Chinese culture also didn't receive any boost to their creativity. Despite the fairly immersive multimedia taster of Chinese culture (which was relatively alien to these Midwestern American students), this group didn't perform any better on the test of creativity either.

Both the dual American and Chinese culture presentation as well as the fusion American–Chinese culture presentation boosted creativity, providing evidence that exposure to unfamiliar cultures can improve creativity. But why did the dual culture presentation and the hybrid culture presentation boost creativity when the presentation focused purely on Chinese culture did not?

Perhaps mere exposure to a new culture – or indeed any new ideas or knowledge – isn't enough to boost creativity. We get the benefits of such experience only when we actively engage with new concepts or information. When the study participants simply sat through the presentation about Chinese culture, they had little reason to relate what they were seeing and hearing to what they already knew. The 100 per cent Chinese presentation was too alien, too foreign for them to relate to and assimilate. It was too easy for them to disengage their minds and simply let the experience wash over them.

However, when participants watched slides of American culture interspersed with slides about Chinese culture, their mental machinery may have been forced to link the material together. The participants had more incentive to compare the two cultures, look for commonalities or clashes, and process what they were experiencing at a deeper level. Similarly, when participants were exposed to the fusion of American–Chinese culture, their minds may have been more engaged. In the words of the study authors, participants in the latter two groups became 'more cognitively complex', heightening their performance on the creativity test.

Taking the results as a whole, the study again points to the fact that creativity comes about as the result of an active decision. Mere contact with a new culture isn't enough to enhance creativity. That explains why even extensive travel in foreign countries doesn't necessarily boost inventive thinking. It's too easy to travel in a bubble that feels like home – to stay at the Hilton or Holiday Inn, eat foods that have been prepared only for tourists' tastes, and get away with few or no words of the local language. To learn from our experiences, we need to take the deliberate decision to engage with a culture, to compare what is similar and what is dissimilar, and relate new experiences back to what we know.

BECOME YOUR BEST: Engaging with experiences

Most of us get more set in our ways as we grow older. We can easily get into ruts of thinking and behaving. For example, I know plenty of people who – despite being only in their thirties or forties – say that they 'don't like the idea of social networking websites', 'can't be bothered with fashion', or 'don't like reality television'. When people say they don't like or can't be bothered to find out about whole categories, that to me is a worrying sign of a closed mind.

Awe is about developing our creativity by exposing ourselves to new situations and sensations, and learning new things. However, simply accumulating experiences and facts is not Awe. Putting ourselves in new situations or cramming novel information into our brains won't necessarily boost our ingenuity unless we actively engage with what we're experiencing. We need to process the information, make connections, and make deductions and predictions and guesses about what we come across.

So read a magazine article about a new topic but be sure to consider how it challenges your perceptions or corroborates what you already know. Go to a restaurant and sample an unfamiliar dish, but avoid simply letting the tastes and smells wash over you. Think about other dishes it reminds you of or the words you would choose to describe it to a friend. Visit a gallery or museum, attend a contemporary dance show or experimental jazz performance, and try to find even a single way in which it might inspire a better way of doing things at home or work.

Don't just take photos when you visit a different town, city, or country. Consider how the architecture differs and think about how local conditions may have influenced how people dress or behave. Don't just observe cultural nuances and conventions; compare them to the norms you've seen elsewhere and allow yourself to wonder how the differences might have come about.

Awe is about active engagement, about questioning, speculating, and thinking about the situations and sensations we experience. Do that, and you may become more creative, more innovative both at home and work.

There's more good news from the Leung and Chiu study too. Five days later, the researchers dragged the volunteers back into their laboratory to complete a second, different test of creativity. Before taking the test, the investigators urged the participants to remind themselves of the presentations they had seen, giving them blank sheets of paper to write down whatever thoughts came to mind about the slide shows.

Again, previous exposure to only American culture or only Chinese culture did not help participants to beat the control group on this new creativity test. However, both the dual cultures and fusion cultures groups performed equally strongly on the creativity test, demonstrating that the 45-minute presentations had an effect that lasted for nearly a week.

Engaging with fresh experiences heightens original thinking. Even if you only manage to do something new once a week, the effects may last the whole week.

Getting better ideas out

So far we've looked at ways to feed the mind and jump-start more elegant ideas. But another vital part of the Awe equation is making time to let those ideas out. So how do people do it?

Tom Mercer is the founder and managing director of mOma (pronounced 'mom-a', not 'moe-ma'), a food company selling healthy breakfast products such as pots of oats soaked in organic apple juice with fruits swirled into yoghurt. The products are available both directly to commuters through stalls at major train stations and indirectly through retailers.

Since opening in 2006, mOma has already grown to become a multimillion-pound business serving the south-east of England; it's also on the cusp of becoming a nationwide success. But back in late 2005, Tom had been working as a junior management consultant at Bain & Company. Where did the idea for the products and his business come from?

Solving the Duncker candle problem

Only about 50 per cent of people identify the right answer to the Duncker quandary. The correct solution is to empty the box of tacks and then affix the box to the wall with the tacks. You can then put the candle inside the box so that any beads of wax stay inside the box rather than dripping on either the floor or table.

The Duncker puzzle is considered a classic measure of creativity because it tests the ability to see objects as performing functions different from how they may typically be used. So the box may be used not only to hold tacks but also as a tray for the candle.

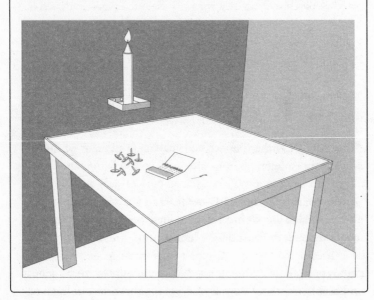

'I knew I wanted to do something, to run my own business. It was all approached on a logical basis, not a "Eureka!" moment or because I was a passionate foodie or anything like that,' he tells me.

He says that he doesn't think of himself as a particularly creative person. Rather than waiting for creative inspiration to strike, he began a conscious process of collecting ideas.

'The times I found best to get the creative juices flowing were walking down Oxford Street, walking down Regent Street, strolling around and being stimulated by everything around and using that to think, to be imaginative, and dream and think of different possibilities of what could be,' Mercer says.

He began talking to friends too, and mining them for ideas. For example, he considered setting up a made-to-measure suit business. He toyed with an idea for a dry-cleaning business aimed at frazzled business executives and then a broader concierge service too. And because his father had been a farmer, he began looking into food-related ideas.

'I looked into smoothies, smoothie bars, hog roasts, and bringing more authentic, traditional, hearty food into central London.'

Eventually, his many conversations and pavement-pounding helped him to reach a realisation.

'If you come into central London, there's a huge amount on offer for lunch and dinner but very little for breakfast. Most of what's on offer for breakfast is lunchtime destinations that tack on a breakfast offering. Wouldn't it be great to do something that was exclusively breakfast that could enable me to focus on breakfast without having to develop lunchtime and evening offerings too?'

And so his idea was born. Mercer's first product was essentially a smoothie with oats added to it, churned to make a porridge-like meal in a bottle. He began selling it outside a train station from a stand converted from an old filing cabinet. Since then, mOma has expanded through partnership deals with retailers such as Waitrose and airline Virgin Atlantic.

Mercer's business inspiration came not because he was innately gifted with creativity but because he invested the time and effort to work on it. He walked around the city, deliberately looking for ideas. He talked to people he knew and trusted. He approached the problem of generating a novel business concept as a task like any other.

Sure, there are accounts of famous 'Eureka!' or 'Aha!' moments in history when scientists or entrepreneurs came up with incredible insights seemingly spontaneously. But, for the most part, we need to make a conscious decision to deploy our creativity; we need to put time into our diaries to consider whether there might be new, better ways of solving problems.

The truth about brainstorming

Suppose you and a posse of friends or colleagues have to come up with a novel solution, an original idea, or a new way of tackling an intractable problem. How would you go about it? Perhaps you'd consider brainstorming, which is, after all, probably the most famous and widely used method for promoting creative thinking in the world.

It's a shame traditional brainstorming is fatally flawed though. Far from promoting creativity, it actually *decreases* it. Fact. So what's going on? And what's the alternative?

Let's start at the beginning with a recap of the basic rules of brainstorming:

- Express any ideas that come to mind
- Generate as many ideas as you can
- Do not criticise any ideas

You've probably sat in a brainstorming session yourself or know people who swear by the technique. When advertising executive Alex Osborn first came up with the concept of brainstorming, he claimed that groups following his guidelines should be twice as productive as similar numbers of individuals.[22]

In a seminal study, Professor Paul Paulus at the University of Texas at Arlington set out to test Osborn's prediction by assigning 80 experimental volunteers to either real groups of four or nominal groups of four.[23] The real groups were prompted to come up with ideas to a problem for 25 minutes while sat together around a table. The nominal groups of four were split up, with the four individuals asked to generate ideas alone while sat in four separate rooms. The researchers then totalled the number of unique ideas (i.e. ones that were not also suggested by anyone else) that the nominal groups came up with to compare the value of brainstorming alone versus in a pack.

Their conclusion? Individuals working alone on average generated 65 per cent more unique ideas than real brainstorming groups.

It's a pretty startling revelation. Across the world, there are hundreds if not thousands of teams and groups gathering to brainstorm every day. But the effectiveness of brainstorming is a total myth.

Research teams from around the world have delved into the field and come up with likely reasons why traditional brainstorming doesn't work. For a start, people edit what they're willing to blurt out in a crowd. The rules of brainstorming urge groups to welcome ideas no matter how silly they might at first seem. In practice, however, people don't want to look stupid in front of friends and colleagues so they self-censor their most outrageous (and perhaps most valuable) ideas.

But the greater issue is that people hit 'verbal traffic jams'. Because only one person can speak at a time, other people may actually forget their ideas when they're listening to someone else speaking. It sounds ridiculous to think that we would forget our sublime ideas but, in the heat of a quick-fire exchange, research shows that it does indeed happen.

Research crews from different institutions have come to the same conclusions about the ineffectiveness of brainstorming. Despite the ongoing belief of people all over the world about the benefits of brainstorming, research tells us that groups of people are significantly less creative than nominal groups of people working individually. Brainstorming groups spawn fewer ideas than individuals working independently; those ideas are also rated by experts as being poorer in quality too.[24] Make no mistake: traditional group brainstorming is fundamentally broken.

Yet people continue to brainstorm collectively rather than on their own. Why?

Probably because they *enjoy* throwing ideas around together. Perhaps the fact that brainstorming in groups can feel effortless and fun is evidence that it isn't terribly effective. I've already argued that generating ideas takes conscious effort. Being creative should be hard work. And the fact that we prefer the ease of group brainstorming sessions to sitting quietly and working on our own should illustrate that collective brainstorming isn't necessarily the best way to maximise our creative thinking.

The 4-TIER approach

So if traditional brainstorming isn't terribly effective, what *does* work? We can still generate new ideas and imagine crazy possibilities. However, we also need to sift and review the ideas we can take forward and use. Based on research and practice, I've come up with a definitive method for idea generation, which I call the 4-TIER approach, because there are four steps: training, inscribing, engaging, and reviewing.

I worked with a creative team at an advertising agency to inject some life into their brainstorming sessions using the 4-TIER approach. We scheduled the session at five o'clock and explained that we'd bring in pizza and beer at five-thirty. Until the goodies arrived, the creative director introduced the objectives for the session. I then ran through the rules of brainstorming (Step 1: training) and urged everyone to spend just 15 minutes writing down ideas individually (Step 2: inscribing). The arrival of the hot pizza and cold beer couldn't help but get the discussion going (Step 3: engaging). About 45 minutes later, we encouraged the gang to evaluate the ideas and choose the best ones to adopt (Step 4: reviewing), which took about 90 minutes.

Having fun and putting in the hard mental effort required to produce genuine originality are not mutually exclusive. Especially if pizza and beer are involved!

Step 1: training

Brainstorming is arguably the world's most popular technique for generating creative ideas. And, if used as *part* of an overall idea-generation process, it can work well. But just because it's well known doesn't mean people necessarily adhere to the

BECOME YOUR BEST: (Re)introducing the rules of brainstorming

I've tried different sets of instructions over the years. Here's a comprehensive set – feel free to photocopy these pages to use as a handout.[25]

1. **Aim for quantity.** The greater the number of ideas we generate, the more the quality usually goes up too. Let's aim for as many ideas as we can.

2. **Go wild.** No idea is too crazy. Don't be afraid to say anything that comes to mind. Outrageous ideas can often spark other, better ideas.

3. **Ban criticism.** Most people find it easier to put down an idea than to come up with a good idea of their own. No one is allowed to criticise. We'll review and evaluate ideas only after we've finished generating ideas.

4. **Combine and improve.** Look for ways to blend ideas that have already been suggested. Expand, modify, or exaggerate earlier ideas in different ways.

5. **Stay focused.** Concentrate on coming up with ideas. Avoid telling stories about your experiences and feel free to remind other people not to tell stories either! Don't let people explain why they think their idea is a good one. Sharing the idea is enough; they can explain why they like their own ideas later.

6. **Build on what we've got.** If you feel you're running out of ideas, take a look back at the ideas we've already come up with and aim to extend or build on those previous ones.

rules. A good start is usually to set some guidelines and remind people of the principles with just two minutes of basic training (see box).

Another reason that groups may underperform has been dubbed social loafing.[26] When people know that their efforts are going to be pooled, some individuals may decide – either unconsciously or consciously – to put in less effort because they think they can get away with it.

I suggest introducing an element of competition to beat the loafing tendency. I usually bring along a prize like a bottle of champagne. Or, if the gang is cosy and gets on well, ask everyone to chip in a small amount of money – perhaps a low-denomination note. Explain that the whole cash pot will go to the person who is voted as having generated the greatest *number* of ideas – regardless of their quality. Especially in competitive groups, that usually raises the quantity (and, ultimately, the quality) of ideas generated.

Step 2: inscribing
The next step isn't actually to generate ideas as a group. No matter how we look at it, we can't get away from the fact that groups continue to underperform nominal groups made up of individuals working on their own.

So Step 2 is to plead with people to work on their own – at least for a little while. Nicknamed brain*writing*, the aim is to get people to share ideas by writing them on sheets of paper and passing them along to others within the group.[27] Trials show that brainwriting groups of four people outperform both brainstorming groups and nominal groups of individuals working alone who don't share their ideas[28] – this effect is especially powerful if people work individually before coming together as a group rather than the other way around.[29] If you have more than four people in your group, then divide your participants into a couple of smaller syndicates of no more than four people.

One cunning trick is to ask people to write in different coloured pens so that they are more aware of who spawned which ideas. It makes people feel more accountable and helps to push up both the quality and quantity of ideas.

BECOME YOUR BEST: Kicking off with brainwriting

I usually introduce brainwriting by saying: 'We will soon begin our brainstorming discussion. However, research shows that working individually significantly ratchets up both the quantity and quality of ideas, so we will start off by writing down some of our ideas silently.' I usually present the following instructions as a short handout:[30]

- You will write your ideas on sheets of paper and share these amongst each other. Please avoid talking while doing this. Use simple words and phrases. Don't worry about spelling or grammar.

- You will each use a different colour pen to write one idea on a sheet of paper, which you will pass on to the person on your immediate right.

- You will then receive the sheet of paper from the person on your left. Read the idea(s) on the sheet of paper, write your next idea on it, and pass it on to the right.

- If you finish writing your idea and have yet to receive another sheet of paper, you may write any additional ideas on further blank sheets of paper.

- When you receive the sheet of paper you started on, simply put it in a pile at the centre of the table.

Step 3: engaging

Scribbling ideas on pieces of paper may be effective, but it isn't necessarily that much fun. People like sharing their thoughts, shouting ideas out, and interacting with each other. By allowing people in Step 3 to engage with each other, we get a respectable trade-off between generating a sufficient number of ideas and having a bit of fun.

Now's the time for a chunk of traditional brainstorming, for throwing ideas in and talking over each other. Remember that the rules of brainstorming still apply though. Just because the gates have opened for discussion doesn't mean that criticism is allowed – yet!

Step 4: reviewing

Steps 2 and 3 focus on generating lots and lots of ideas. This final step allows us to review the many ideas and decide which one(s) to take forward.

Even here, most groups need guidance because too many people think that evaluating ideas should be done quickly. Most human beings seem to have a need for certainty – to find just one 'right' answer as rapidly as they can. Everyone's a critic. We can all sneer at modern art, new buildings, films, music, products, or ideas we don't like. But it takes real genius to evaluate ideas constructively and draw out what's positive or helpful about them.

BECOME YOUR BEST: Evaluating ideas effectively

People can become so negative that they see only weaknesses and limitations wherever they look, dismissing ideas in quick succession without giving considered thought to how they could be refined, developed, or turned into profitable ideas. Here are four rules for reviewing ideas usefully: [31]

- **Practise affirmative judgement.** No, this doesn't mean praising every idea. But switch to a constructive lens through which to evaluate ideas. Begin by asking, 'What's good about this idea? What are its advantages or strengths?' rather than rejecting ideas immediately. Even when you come across limitations or problems, try to phrase your doubts as questions, such as, 'How could we...?' rather than killing ideas off.

- **Consider both novelty and feasibility.** We could apply many criteria to judging ideas. But it often helps to consider both novelty (i.e. 'To what extent is this an original idea?') and feasibility (i.e. 'How does it move us closer towards our goals?'). The most potent ideas are likely to be high on both novelty and feasibility.

- **Give explicit reasons.** Be sure to explain why you either support or disapprove of an idea. We can easily fall into the trap of assuming that the reasons are obvious. Whenever you express an opinion, be sure to answer the question 'Why?' out loud.

- **Keep your end goal in sight.** The biggest trap many people fall into is that they focus too quickly on showing their disapproval of ideas, whereas people at the opposite end of the spectrum occasionally get too excited with the open-ended, blue-sky, off-course nature of brainstorming. Remember that Step 4 is about reviewing ideas and looking for an idea or perhaps a handful of options to take forward. Keep an eye on the clock to ensure that the four-step 4-TIER session produces useful outputs.

Brainraining

Occasionally, when we don't want a big storm, perhaps a sprinkle of light rain will do. Full-blown brainstorming requires a lot of work. But that doesn't mean that we can't apply the same principles on a smaller scale even when we are trying to think more creatively on our own.

All we need to do is take a few seconds to reignite our sense of Awe. Taking the time to pause and ask ourselves a few questions can help us to think more creatively and perhaps summon forth better solutions and ways of doing things.

Try this. Simply work through five questions:

- What's the rational course of action?

- What's the emotional thing to do?

- What would the cleverest person you know – someone you like and respect – do?

- What would your most compassionate friend do?

- Finally, what should you do?

Having Awe-some kids

A friend's son, Joseph, is fairly typical of most teenagers, spending most of his time glued to his computer. Sure, he posts updates to Facebook that are sure to annoy adults who are sticklers for spelling and grammar ('heyy ad guud time bin swimming but lukin 4ward 2 par-T l8r n no skwl tmoz'). He's also teaching himself how to design customised icons for his Bebo webpage that link to his favourite TV shows, bands, and idols.

His parents could tell him off for wasting time on his computer rather than doing his history homework. But they don't. Far from it, they even encourage it.

At first it confused me. Both of his parents have doctorates – one is a nuclear physicist and the other a university lecturer in zoology. For two people who are so seriously loaded with academic qualifications, aren't they afraid their son is going to turn into a school dropout?

I didn't have the guts to voice the question, but then a new thought hit me. Who's to say what's better for Joseph's future – studying long-dead kings and queens or honing his computer expertise?

Educating the next generation isn't the same as getting them to pass exams. Plenty of entrepreneurs, leaders, and entertainers attained bombastic success despite dropping out of school or university – such as Richard Branson and Walt Disney, and photographer Annie Leibovitz, to name but three. Many of the exceptional people I interviewed for this book didn't do well within the confines of a traditional schooling either.

The world has changed so much since you and I were children and will continue to change at an ever more furious pace. No one – not governments, teachers, so-called futurologists, nor you and I – can predict what is on the horizon. We can't say what technological, sociological, and medical advances may happen. Our kids may end up applying breakthroughs that have yet to be made in jobs that we can't even imagine. They might become nuclear fusion engineers, nanobot builders, neuropsychological entertainers, pilots on the Lunar-Martian Express, underwater seaweed farmers, thought police – you get the idea.

To help younger generations to prepare, we must ensure that they *enjoy* learning. They must learn the joy and value of learning rather than simply memorising facts that we currently believe are important. Stuffing knowledge into their heads isn't the same as inspiring them to learn for the rest of their lives.

Rather than simply teaching them, we must encourage them to find the answers themselves. If you want to instil in children a love of learning rather than the accumulation of knowledge, be sure to ask them: 'What do you think?', 'What do we already know that might help us answer that?' and 'How could we find out?'

Onwards and upwards

Awe is the ability to make time for curiosity, inquisitiveness, and wonderment about the world. We can come up with powerful new ideas and occasionally incredible ways of doing things when we carve out time in our busy schedules to learn and ponder. Consider the small changes you could make to help you achieve your creative potential:

- We may fail to spot opportunities if we focus too intently on the tasks we have to do. Remember to make time to activate your sense of Awe; remind yourself to consider what's possible so you can spot useful ideas and make better decisions.

- Remember that little knowledge can be considered fixed and unchangeable. Make time to keep abreast of developments not only in your particular topic but likewise seemingly unrelated fields.

- Aim to link new experiences to what you already know. We get the most benefit from experiences when we make a conscious effort to engage with and question what we're observing, learning, or encountering.

- Aim to work smart rather than hard. Thinking and considering options can often pay dividends much more than taking action immediately. Whether you have hours to brainstorm fresh ideas or only 60 seconds to consider alternative options, you may be more productive in the long term.

TWO

CHERISHING

'*The most important thing in communication is to hear what isn't being said.*'

Peter Drucker

JOHNNY ROXBURGH THROWS PARTIES for a living. To say Roxburgh throws a good party is like saying that Madonna is fairly well known or Albert Einstein was quite clever. As co-founder of events company The Admirable Crichton, he jets around the globe organising astounding parties for both wealthy individuals and corporate clients such as Ralph Lauren and Louis Vuitton.

He remains tight-lipped over his private clients. But the fact that the business holds a royal warrant and regularly orchestrates events for the Queen, Prince Charles and Prince William means that the company is in high demand amongst the world's most moneyed individuals. Roxburgh lets slip that he recently catered a party with a budget of £3 million.

So, what do you get at one of his events? At a party in Marrakesh, he created a nearly invisible dance floor on the surface of a swimming pool. By using cleverly painted support rods beneath a transparent acrylic floor, he allowed 60 guests to believe they were twirling on the surface of the pool itself. Of course the 20-piece orchestra was similarly deposited on the shimmering waters. The effect was so seamless that he had to build a safety rail around the edges of the dance floor to prevent revellers from accidentally plunging into the pool.

Listening to him speak about other parties in St Petersburg, Zurich, and Aspen, Colorado, I don't doubt that Roxburgh is blessed with a fertile, creative mind and an eye for detail. But his success is perhaps less to do with his imagination and more to do with his ability to read and relate to people.

'Ultimately people buy people,' Roxburgh tells me. 'If you have two people pitching for the same job, the person that bonds with the client will win.'

He tells me about an occasion when he pitched to handle the wedding for one of the richest men in Europe. He flew to the Swiss home of the man and his wife-to-be but was surprised to find another wedding planner had also been invited to dine with the couple. Within minutes, Roxburgh had read the client and knew how to behave.

'Whenever the other planner suggested something, I said, "That's a really clever idea, well done," not in a patronising way, but I was very positive. Whenever I suggested something, he said, "People have done that before." He put me down the whole time and I didn't react at all,' he recounts.

He also made an effort to maintain eye contact with his host throughout the dinner. 'There's nothing more disarming than looking another human being smack in the eyes and smiling. If you look at someone in the eyes and smile, it is physically impossible for them not to smile back. We're monkeys, we're programmed to do that.'

Needless to say: Roxburgh won the pitch.

'I don't think my ideas were more or less creative. I hadn't even formulated them. That was people buying people,' he explains.

Putting people at the heart of all he does extends to every one of his vast armies of employees too. In 2004, he was asked by the Greek Olympic Committee to coordinate two parties for dignitaries and heads of state visiting the Athens games. He flew a team of more than 100 employees to Greece to run the festivities. On a rare day off between the two events, one of his team was tragically killed in a car accident.

Several of his colleagues saw him die; many of the team were highly shaken up, putting the second event in jeopardy.

Roxburgh's immediate thoughts were not about the event but the welfare of his team, the employees he sees as part of his extended family. He gave them all the option of staying to run the event or returning home to the UK. For the ones who were too distraught to stay, he paid for business-class tickets and limousines to return them to their homes.

Roxburgh is used to dealing with royalty and billionaires, but for the few hours I spend with him, I feel like the centre of the universe. At several points during our interview, his BlackBerry vibrates quietly on his desk. I glance at it, wondering if he will take the calls. He doesn't. His eye contact is unwavering. He continues speaking in his low, calm voice. The message he conveys is that he is committed to helping me with the research for this book. Nothing short of an earthquake will stop him from giving me the full weight of his attention.

He admits that putting himself into the shoes of other people is not a knack that comes automatically. 'I often don't do it. I lost a job last week because I hadn't established what the client's priority was,' he confesses.

No one can be perfectly attuned 100 per cent of the time to the needs of other people. When Roxburgh gets it right, he gets it very right. As the lead salesperson for his company, he has turned wealthy clients into fast friends and, in doing so, built a multimillion-pound business. He is a noble example of what anyone can achieve by making an unrelenting effort to appreciate the world from another person's perspective.

People skills

Cherishing is a flair for rapport building, for building relationships with other people. High achievers are usually great at listening to others, considering their perspectives and empathising with them; they are respectful of the differences between people and seek emotional connections or personal bonds rather than just making demands for what they want.

We've always needed to put ourselves into the shoes of other people. Sure, a father could chide his daughter for not having done her homework and order her to do it, but he will be so much more effective in persuading her if he takes the time to figure out why she's not doing her studies. A boss who gets to know the team and wins their trust will get them working harder than they would if he or she simply barked instructions at them. A husband who can read the conflicted emotions crossing his wife's face has a much better chance of a long and happy marriage.

In the past, we used to call such abilities 'people skills' or 'social skills'. In recent years, writer Daniel Goleman has popularised the term 'emotional intelligence'.[32] I know one organisation that calls it, somewhat cumbersomely, 'social-emotional agility'.

Whatever the label we attach to it, the need for Cherishing is only growing. In years gone by, we used to work much more locally, perhaps moving to our nearest large town or city to find employment. We tended to work with people with similar educational backgrounds, the same religion, and even the same skin colour. But that's no longer the case as globalisation gains pace.

As the most talented and ambitious people increasingly cross geographic and cultural borders in search of the best opportunities, we find ourselves living and working in ever more diverse communities.[33] We can't expect that a 20-year-old Russian student, 73-year-old Scottish grandmother or 55-year-old Indian entrepreneur will think the same way as we do when we work with them or live with them. Certainly, if we want to influence such people, get them to buy from us, or simply live in harmony with them, we cannot take for granted many of the social conventions and rules we're used to.

Thankfully, we all have the ability to intuit what's going on in other people's heads, to take their perspectives, and empathise with them. And once we understand their thoughts and feelings and have insight into what makes them tick, we can open up new avenues for smoothing over disagreements, building effective relationships, and finding stronger ways of working together.

We're not born with the ability, but it develops in us from a very early age. Sadly, having an ability isn't always the same as using it – or using it accurately. To explain, let me take you through the story of how our minds mature in early childhood.

The puzzle of the ball in the box

Whether you have children of your own or not, imagine the following scenario. A couple of friends beg you to look after their two young children, Amy and Billy, one Saturday afternoon. Your friends are extraordinarily cautious parents; they say that they don't want their children hurting themselves on any sharp edges. And they'd hate for their children to damage any of your lovely furniture, so they suggest you move everything out of the room where they'll be playing.

It's a strange request, but you agree and strip the room bare. All you leave behind for them to play with are a cardboard box, a plastic bucket, and a rubber ball. It doesn't look particularly inviting but that's what your friends want.

It's Saturday afternoon and the kids arrive. Moments after waving their parents goodbye, Amy and Billy rush in to play with the ball, passing it backwards and forwards and kicking it around. After a few minutes, Amy says she's thirsty. You tell her you poured them both some lemonade – in plastic tumblers, of course – in the kitchen. Billy doesn't want a drink, so Amy puts the ball into the box before running through into the kitchen. While she's out of sight in the kitchen gulping down her drink, Billy reaches into the box. He takes the ball and drops it into the bucket before his sister gets back.

So here's a question for you: when Amy returns from the kitchen, where will she look for the ball? Clearly, that's not a gruelling question for you. But consider instead if you were to ask Billy: 'Where do you think Amy will look for the ball?' What would he tell you?

It's a bit of a trick question. The answer depends on Billy's age.

Most three-year-olds can't distinguish between what they know and what other people know. So a three-year-old Billy, knowing that the ball is in the bucket, would guess wrongly and say that Amy would look in the bucket too. He never considers that what he knows and what other people know could be different.

However, by the age of four or five, most children begin to grasp that other people can have different thoughts and beliefs. So a five-year-old Billy would probably answer that Amy would look for the ball in the box where she left it originally. Older and wiser, he is able to separate what he knows from Amy's lack of knowledge, her false belief about the ball's location.

This ability to understand that other people can have knowledge that differs from our own has been dubbed a 'theory of mind' by psychologists – it's considered a theory insofar as the concept of a mind isn't something we can observe directly.[34] We can't see other people's minds, touch them, or examine them until we're satisfied that other people definitely have them.

We can only infer that other people have minds through a combination of introspection and the assumption that other people must possess minds similar to our own. Growing up as children, we gradually became aware that we had thoughts, feelings, and knowledge that other people didn't always know about. Then, by watching the behaviour of the people around us, we came to realise that other people must have thoughts, feelings, and knowledge – in other words, minds – like us too.

I say that most children over the age of four can separate what they know from what other people know. But that's not always the case. Even adults sometimes fail to make this vital distinction too.

The curse of knowledge

As grown-ups, we possess the mental capacity to take another person's perspective and consider their thoughts and feelings. So surely we wouldn't make the same mistakes as children, right?

Suppose you've been invited to take part in an experiment, which will take the form of a two-person game. Cash-strapped university students take part in research studies like this all over the world, so imagine you find yourself sitting in a waiting room with a fellow volunteer called Jenny.

A researcher shows up, ushering you and Jenny into a room where you see a 4-by-4 array of pigeonholes set up on a table. 11 of the pigeonholes are open at both ends, but 5 of the pigeonholes have been closed off at one end. The researcher seats you in front of the pigeonholes so you can see into all 16 holes; the researcher seats Jenny behind it so she can only see into 11 of the holes.

The researcher puts a blindfold on Jenny and then places eight objects into the pigeonholes. Six of the objects are different, but two are identical: children's building blocks with the letter R on them. One of the blocks is in an uncovered slot so Jenny can see it; the other is in a covered slot so she can't see it.

The researcher removes Jenny's blindfold and explains that she must give you instructions to move objects around the grid. So if Jenny tells you to 'move the toy car one space up', that's what you must do. Straightforward enough.

And so the experiment begins. Jenny says: 'Move the cup one space to my left.' Remembering that her left is your right, you move the cup one space to your right.

'Move the bottle one space to my left.' Easy enough. You move the bottle to your right.

'Now move the building block up one space.'

Which building block? There are two. But then you recall that Jenny was blindfolded and can't know about the second building block. And the realisation hits you. You've figured out the twist in the experiment. The researcher wants to test whether you'll reach for the building block that both you and Jenny can see or the one that only you know about.

Of course you're not going to fall into that trap. You may even feel slightly indignant that a researcher would believe you capable of making such a rudimentary mistake. Surely no one would reach for the wrong object!

But when researcher Boaz Keysar at the University of Chicago used an almost identical version of the test, he found that 30 per cent of participants attempted to move the wrong item.[35] When he repeated the experiment three more times, he found that 71 per cent of participants reached for the incorrect item at least once. In other words, more than two in three people forgot that they had information that differed from that of their experimental partners.

Psychologists call this the curse of knowledge. Once we are 'cursed' by knowledge about something, we find it tough to put ourselves into the shoes of people who lack that knowledge. We know that the capital of France is Paris, so how could anyone possibly *not* know? If we're experts at writing business plans or changing diapers, we forget that others may struggle to do the same or never learned how to in the first place.

Most modern mobile phones have the technological capacity to surf the Internet, although the truth is that many people choose not to use the function at all. In a similar fashion, even though we have the mental capacity to take the conceptual perspective of another person, we don't always use it. We forget to switch the ability on.

The fact that we don't always take the perspectives of other people into account shouldn't surprise anyone. We've all made assumptions or jumped to the wrong conclusions based on limited facts. When we know a fact, we subconsciously believe that it must be apparent or even obvious to our friends or colleagues too. Especially when we're tired or under pressure, we forget that other people possess knowledge and opinions that may differ from our own. As the cliché says, when we ASSUME, we make an ASS out of U and ME.

The curse of knowledge isn't only limited to the information we know. Whatever our opinions, values, or even emotions, we may assume that others feel the same way too. A parent who is outraged by the lack of childcare places at a local nursery may take for granted that everyone else in the area would be equally incensed by the issue. A senior manager alarmed by a drop in company profits may presume that front-line employees would be similarly concerned too.

The stronger our views and opinions, the less likely we are to put ourselves into the shoes of other people. So most law-abiding people can't imagine why a gang would vandalise a communal park. Adults can't conceive why kids want to dress themselves in such ridiculous fashions. Individuals with strong political views find it difficult to appreciate the views of people who have the opposite outlook. The more we know or the more strongly we believe, the harder we find it to consider the perspectives of other people.

Remember that we all have the capacity to take other people's perspectives, but often forget to switch it on. The good news is that we can choose to flex our mental muscles and hone our ability.

In another experiment using the 4-by-4 pigeonhole set-up, researchers Shali Wu and Boaz Keysar found that Chinese participants were much better at taking the perspectives of their partners than American subjects. The researchers attributed the differences to the fact that Chinese culture tends to be collectivistic in nature while American culture tends to promote individuality.[36] But the point is that our ability to take the perspectives of other people is not inherent and fixed but learned and changeable.

So get used to putting yourself into other people's shoes. If you're reading this book on a train or in a public place, look around you, or remember to try this next time you are out and about. Pick out a person or two and try to see the world from their point of view. What are they thinking about? What are they feeling at the moment? As with any skill, the more you practise it, the better you get. The more you do it, the more quickly and naturally it will come.

Failing to cherish

I work with a lot of professional services firms: accountants, lawyers, investment bankers, advertising executives, and consultants. They all have in common the fact that their biggest assets are more likely the quality of their people than patents or proprietary technologies.

One particular management consulting firm picks some of the most academically gifted, internationally educated people to be its consultants. The firm – I'll call it Bright Sparks – has many hundreds of consultants based out of over a dozen offices spanning the globe and works with some of the world's biggest brand-name companies. The partners regularly take home half a million each year. Even young graduate recruits earn nearly three times as much as the average graduate.

Yet not all is well. While Bright Sparks is continuing to win business with new clients, their new projects are masking a decline elsewhere. When pitching to existing client organisations for repeat business, the partners at Bright Sparks have noticed that they're losing out more and more to one particular competitor. Alarmingly and slightly embarrassingly, the partners view this rival as being a strictly second-tier firm. The consultants at this second firm – I'll call it Nearly As Clever Consulting – are still well educated and well paid, but certainly not to the world-class standards of the consultants at Bright Sparks.

What's going on? Why is Nearly As Clever Consulting gaining ground on Bright Sparks?

I mentioned that Bright Sparks hires people who are much more the academic elite than the employees at Nearly As Clever Consulting. Let me give you an idea of what I mean by profiling a consultant from each firm.

First, someone from Bright Sparks: Alastair Poulter excelled at almost everything he studied at school, passing his exams with ease and usually coming top of his year. No one was surprised when he won a place to study at Magdalen College, University of Oxford, where he felt right at home with some of the smartest students in the country. On graduating with a first-class degree in history and economics, he got a job in the London office of Bright Sparks. The firm received over 500 applications and took on only six analysts that year, all of whom came from either Oxford or Cambridge universities.

After working there for three years, Poulter's bosses encouraged him to pursue an MBA. They were so impressed by his future potential that they paid all of his tuition fees – a sum amounting to tens of thousands of pounds – on the condition that he return to work for the firm. He gained a place at Harvard Business School and, after two years of study, returned to Bright Sparks to continue working as a consultant alongside other clever folks plucked from the premier league of academic institutions from around the world. At the age of 27, he already earns six figures a year.

Jennifer Reeves, on the other hand, did well at school but wasn't by any means the best performer. She got good grades in her school exams and was pleased to go to the University of Exeter to study business studies and German. On graduating with a second-class degree, she wanted a career in consulting too and applied to Bright Sparks. She didn't even get offered an interview. At the same time, she applied to Nearly As Clever Consulting and was offered a job as an analyst in their London office. Nearly As Clever Consulting took on nearly 500 graduates that year. After working there for four years, she was promoted to become a manager, looking after teams of up to five or six younger analysts at a time. At the age of 27, she earns £68,000 a year.

Intellectually speaking, there's almost no comparison between Poulter and Reeves either. In casual conversation, Reeves references pop culture, for example her liking for the television shows *Top Gear* and *Crime Scene Investigation*. Poulter, on the other hand, says that he doesn't own a television because he 'doesn't believe in it'. His attempts at chit-chat include multiple literary references; he asks pointed questions such as: 'Have you read Karl Marx's *Critique of Hegel's "Philosophy of Right"*?'

Whether intentionally or not, Poulter conveys that he's the kind of clever person who prefers literary works over lowbrow television. But given that Bright Sparks' client organisations are filled with the kinds of regular people who probably watch TV rather than poring over obscure classics, I imagine that their clients notice the intellectual gulf and feel somewhat ill at ease.

The same pattern emerges throughout Bright Sparks. Because their consultants come from such a rarefied minority, they are always sharper than their clients. When Bright Sparks consutants get together, they talk about how their clients don't have the intellectual horsepower to succeed in business. When their clients don't – or can't – follow their recommendations, the Bright Sparks team secretly roll their eyes and mock their clients' failings.

Being scholarly superstars, the Bright Sparks consultants suffer from the 'curse of knowledge', finding it harder to consider how their decidedly more ordinary clients must feel. They don't make enough of an effort to put themselves into the shoes of their averagely intelligent clients.

On the other hand, the Nearly As Clever Consulting team rarely disparage their clients' brainpower. Rather than seeing their clients as dumb or lazy, they more easily grasp their dilemmas. When clients don't follow their recommendations, the Nearly As Clever Consulting team ask: 'What have *we* done wrong?' and 'How can we engage our clients?' rather than simply accepting the fact their clients aren't clever enough to do what it takes.

So while clients may hire Bright Sparks to work for them once, they often find that they don't click with the Bright Sparks team. While they respect the Bright Sparks consultants for their intellectual calibre, they eventually decide to bring in the Nearly As Clever Consulting team because they feel more *cherished*.

I don't believe that the Bright Sparks team *can't* see the world from their clients' eyes. They simply don't do it often or deeply enough. Many people believe that they regularly put themselves into the shoes of other people. Truth is that we generally do it in a fairly superficial way. Even though I trained as a psychologist, I don't do it as often as I should. We don't spend enough time pondering questions like 'Why might this person think and feel the way they do?' and 'What about this person's culture, background and circumstances might make this person believe and act this way?'

The view from the top

Before I move on, I have a little experiment for you to try. With your dominant hand, as quickly as you can, snap your fingers five times. Go on, do it before we move on. If you're reading this book in a public place, do it quietly, perhaps surreptitiously by your side.

Next, with the same hand, trace a capital letter E on your forehead.

So here's the critical question: did you draw it with the E facing you (as in the left-hand image) or away from you (the right-hand image)?

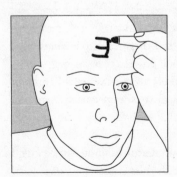 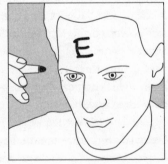

Psychologist Adam Galinsky at Northwestern University used this same task to test the extent to which people consider the perspectives of others, inviting undergraduate students to participate in an experiment for a small cash sum.[37] When they arrived in his laboratory, he assigned them to either a high-power condition or a low-power condition.

In the high-power condition, participants were asked to recall and write about a personal incident in which they had felt a sense of power over another person or group of people. In the low-power condition, participants were requested to write about a personal incident in which someone else had power over them.

After completing the written exercise, the participants were brought individually into a separate room and told by a researcher that they were about to take part in a coordination task. They were told to snap their fingers five times with their dominant hand and to draw a capital letter E on their foreheads with a marker pen.

Galinsky and his team theorised that people in positions of power would be more likely to have an egocentric view of the world and therefore be more likely to draw the letter E in a way that would be backwards to other people (as in the left-hand picture). And that's precisely what the results showed. 33 per cent of the high-power participants scribbled a self-oriented E on their foreheads. Only 12 per cent of the low-power participants drew a self-oriented E on themselves. Simply writing about wielding power over others made participants three times more likely to see the world through their own viewpoint as opposed to the perspective of the researcher in the room.

Okay, so a quick five-minute manipulation of power was enough to swell a crowd of students' heads, their sense of egocentricity.

Big deal. What does that mean for us in the real world?

I find the implications quite scary actually. Imagine how power must affect the viewpoint of real managers, politicians, parents, community leaders, doctors, and other people in positions of authority. When people get used to having sway and influence over others, they may become less and less likely to consider the viewpoint of others. Powerful people could so easily get drawn into a spiral of making decisions that disregard the instincts and views of the people around them.

But there's good news. It's not that people in power *can't* put themselves into the shoes of others – it's simply that they may not *remember* to do so. And so here's the lesson: make a conscious effort to consider the perspectives of other people. The more powerful, the more senior, the more influential you are in the world, the more likely you may be to forget how 'ordinary people' think.

Separating thoughts from feelings

So far I've talked about Cherishing as a single skill, an ability to discern the thoughts and feelings of the people around us. But now I'm going to complicate matters by distinguishing between thinking about others' thoughts versus thinking about their feelings.

Strictly speaking, thinking about other people's thoughts is called perspective-taking; thinking about what other people are feeling is called empathy. When it comes to dealing with other people, which of the two do you think helps us to be more effective?

One research team examined the impact of perspective-taking versus empathy on people's negotiation skills, by asking pairs of MBA students to haggle in a variety of different negotiation scenarios.[38] In the first scenario, one person in each pair was told to act as the buyer and the other to act as a seller of a hypothetical service station. Each was given a week to prepare for the negotiation by working through a pack of instructions and background information about the gas station and their role as either buyer or seller. Making the task tougher for the participants, though, the crafty investigators made it impossible for the buyer and seller to reach an agreement based only on price. Specifically, the buyer was instructed not to pay more than a certain amount of money, a price that happened to be less than the minimum value that the seller was told to accept. A deal could only be reached if the two parties haggled and came to an agreement on a variety of non-financial issues that were hinted at within each of their sets of instructions.

Before the negotiation began, the buyers were split into one of three experimental groups. One group was given special empathy instructions as follows:

'In preparing for the negotiation and during the negotiation, take the perspective of the service-station owner. Try to understand what they are *feeling*, what *emotions* they may be experiencing in selling the station. Try to imagine what you would be *feeling* in that role.'

A second group was given perspective-taking instructions that had a slightly different focus:

'In preparing for the negotiation and during the negotiation, take the perspective of the service-station owner. Try to understand what they are *thinking*, what their *interests* and *purposes* are in selling the station. Try to imagine what you would be *thinking* in that role.'

A third control group was given no additional instructions and told to continue straight into the negotiation. After 50 minutes of furious negotiating, the researchers noticed a distinct pattern; 39 per cent of the control buyers had managed to reach an agreement with their sellers. 54 per cent of the empathy group reached an agreement, but a massive 76 per cent of the perspective-taking group reached an agreement. In other words, a rudimentary set of instructions to consider the *thoughts* rather than the *feelings* of the seller helped buyers to double their chances of reaching a fruitful outcome.

To check that the result wasn't a fluke, the researchers repeated the exercise with a separate group of MBA students and a different scenario. As before, the students were divided into pairs. One person took on the role of an employer looking to hire a candidate but wanting to broker the best deal for the organisation; the other person assumed the role of the candidate, wanting to get the best possible salary and benefit package.

Two minutes prior to beginning the negotiation exercise, participants acting as the employer were again split into one of three groups. In the empathy group, employers were told to imagine what it would *feel like* to be in the situation of the candidate. Employers in the perspective-taking group were told to focus on what the candidate would be *thinking* about. Control participants were given no further instructions.

The key difference between the sets of instructions was again subtle, but the effects were not. Only 12 per cent of the pairs achieved the best possible win-win outcomes in the control condition. Of the pairs given empathy instructions 22 per cent achieved win-win outcomes. And a whopping 40 per cent of the perspective-taking participants achieved win-win outcomes.

Taking both negotiation scenarios together, we can see that empathy has benefits when it comes to dealing with other people. Putting ourselves into the situations of others and imagining how they feel can help us to negotiate more effectively. However, perspective-taking may be even more beneficial. Considering the *thoughts* that other people hold in their heads may have the most benefit of all.

Personally, I'm staggered that such a small change in phrasing can have such a robust impact. Remember that the participants had been given a whole week to prepare. Yet reading three sentences a couple of minutes before the negotiation gave a massive boost to the brokering effectiveness of the perspective-taking participants.

Remember that these were competitive, driven, bright MBA students too. You'd think that they would automatically make the effort to consider the perspectives of the people sat on the other side of the negotiation table. Yet they didn't. Because having the ability to empathise and consider the perspectives of other people doesn't mean that they remembered to switch it on.[39]

To me, it again illustrates that we all have the ability to empathise and consider the perspectives of other people. We just don't always use those abilities. Without prompting, we simply...forget.

We all have the ability to intuit both the feelings and thoughts of others when we choose to. Exceptional people don't necessarily have more of this ability; they may simply remember to switch on their Cherishing skill more of the time. So how can you encourage yourself to use the skill?

Bear in mind that the instructions that the researchers used were very simple. We don't need to overcomplicate matters. Even a few words such as 'Cherish' or 'Consider perspectives' jotted down on a Post-it Note or a diarised task in our online schedules might be enough to kick our Cherishing skills into action more of the time.

The benefits of reminding ourselves to consider the perspectives of others are clear. If we want to be effective in our dealings with other people, we must remember to take their perspectives.

BECOME YOUR BEST: Diving deep into people's psyches

The simple act of reminding ourselves to imagine another person's perspective can give us a great deal of insight into how they see the world, and doing so can prepare us to negotiate and handle interactions with other people more effectively. But sometimes we need more.

Suppose you're not dealing with a run-of-the-mill customer but the crucial one that could make your fortune. Or you've discovered that your teenage daughter has started having sex and you need to have a serious talk with her. When the stakes are high, we may benefit from delving deeper into the instincts and feelings of others.

Several factions of researchers including James Weyant at the University of San Diego have found that a 'day in the life' writing exercise is a winning technique for encouraging people to engage fully with the perspectives of others.[40]

If you can, get a photograph of the person (or people) you're trying to understand better. If you can't get hold of a photo, then try to imagine how the person looks. Then write a short essay – a couple of paragraphs – about a typical day in that person's life *as if you were that person*. Write in the first person, saying, 'I get up in the morning and . . .' or 'When I get to work, the first thing I do is . . .' or 'I feel . . .'. You should use the words 'me' and 'my' to describe your thoughts, feelings, and experiences too.

It's up to you how long you spend on the exercise. I suspect that even a few minutes of frantic scribbling and immersing yourself in someone else's life is better than none. On the other hand, writing pages and pages probably won't help you much more than if you write a few paragraphs.

Remember that this isn't a technique to use every day necessarily. You're a busy person, you have lots to do. But on those singular occasions when you need to understand another person as fully as possible, give it a go.

Embracing both/and rather than either/or

Imagining the world from the perspectives of other people can help us to be more effective in our dealings with them. But the effort of seeing the world through a different viewpoint usually takes us only halfway to where we need to be. Sometimes, even when we know what another person is thinking or feeling, we may still struggle to build a relationship or even rapport with them.

What's your all-time favourite film? Perhaps it's a critically acclaimed masterpiece such as *The Godfather* or *Citizen Kane*? A fan favourite such as *Star Wars* or one of the *Lord of the Rings* trilogy? Or even a feel-good movie such as *It's a Wonderful Life* or *Pretty Woman*? Whatever you like, I can promise you that there's someone out there who hates it.

The same goes for just about anything. Two students can read Leo Tolstoy's classic *Anna Karenina*. He thinks it's delightful. She thinks that the book is overly long and poorly paced.

Faced with an identical stimulus – the same film, book, piece of art, song, whatever – we can come to dramatically different conclusions. So imagine how much more complicated matters can get when we come to our recollection of events.

There's a well-known scene in the film comedy *Annie Hall* in which Woody Allen's character Alvy and Diane Keaton's character Annie are each seeing their therapists. On a split screen, they are quizzed by their therapists about how often they have sex. Alvy laments: 'Hardly ever. Maybe three times a week.' Annie, in an annoyed fashion, replies: 'Constantly. I'd say three times a week.'

Or say you hear about an argument that two married friends had. She says to you that he forgot their anniversary. He keeps working late and spends too much time at the office. He tells you that he's trying to get a promotion, that he wants to earn enough so they can buy their first home together and start a family. Who's right, who's wrong? Maybe both of them?

One of the trickiest challenges we face in life is dealing with conflict – ranging from minor disagreements to furious quarrels. Few people enjoy confrontation, and those who do often tackle it in too aggressive a manner. However, staying quiet and wishing the issue will go away isn't a solution either.

Making matters more difficult, we tend to see the world in black-and-white terms. When we have a difference of opinion, our default is to assume that either 'I'm right (and you're wrong),' or 'You're right (and I'm wrong).' However, the real world doesn't always operate in either/or, black versus white, right versus wrong ways. More often than not, we may need to accept the possibility that we may both be somewhat right at the same time – I can see it one way and you can see it in a different, but equally valid way.

Putting ourselves into the shoes of other people can help to build rapport and understanding. But to cement those bonds, we need to accept that more than one point of view isn't just possible, but likely. When dealing with other people, we can enrich a discussion by exploring how opposing perspectives can be united rather than fought over.

We must learn to accept that, whatever our views and those of the people around us, we may *all* be right – even when those views seem to clash. Don't believe that's possible? Here's a quick arithmetical quiz for you.

What's 1 + 1?

Duh.

2, right?

Not always. Sure, we're taught that 1 + 1 = 2. However, that's only true if we're counting in the base 10 number system. 1 + 1 = 10 if we decide to switch to the base 2 (binary) number system. And 1 + 1 = 1 when we add a further lump of chewing gum to the blob we're already chewing. Or if we put together two animals – say a male and a female mouse – we may come back weeks later to find that 1 + 1 = 9.

The point: even though we may talk about understanding other people's perspectives, we often fall into the trap of only engaging with those other viewpoints in a fairly shallow way. We may be looking for flaws in their arguments to prove us right

BECOME YOUR BEST: Taking the third way

What's the best way to broach that difficult conversation and manage the differences we have with other people? Focus on **both/and** rather than **either/or** thinking. Accept that *both* we and the other person usually feel that we have valid reasons for our behaviour.

A good starting point before initiating any kind of conversation is to assume that both parties have contributed to the situation. This isn't about right versus wrong. In most situations, *both* you *and* the other person may (perhaps unknowingly) have behaved in ways that led to the current situation.

One of the most powerful techniques for resolving differences of opinion is to accept that there are *three* perspectives to any disagreement, *three* sides to the story. There's your perspective, the perspective of the other person, *and* a third perspective that integrates parts from both individual stories – the view that people who don't know either of you might see.

Before you raise an issue with anyone, figure out what that third perspective might be. Imagine that the actions of both yourself and the other party are being filmed by hidden TV cameras. Suppose an impartial observer – perhaps a TV newsreader, a psychologist, or a judge in a court – is trying to describe the story from as objective a viewpoint as possible. What would that neutral onlooker say?

By finding the third perspective, we can adjust the tone of how we broach the discussion. Rather than seeing it as a problem with someone else, we can phrase it as a *difference* between two people, which is usually a less judgemental and more helpful starting point. The more certain we feel that we are backed up by the facts and are 'right', the more helpful this technique can be. Considering the third perspective helps us to broach conversations in a neutral manner, helping us to forgo the kind of fault-finding tone that can make us appear as if we're looking for someone to blame.

and them wrong. But that's not the approach that exceptional people take. No. Instead, exceptional individuals look for ways in which we can all be right.

For an example of how to take the 'third way', suppose I think that a colleague, Penelope, has been turning up to internal meetings consistently late. I feel that the facts are on my side. I have witnesses that she has been late several times. But simply telling her she's been late and that I expect better implies that it's a problem with her that needs fixing. A more fruitful approach would be to phrase it in neutral terms, as a situation that needs resolving with both of our inputs.

Until I explore the issues, I can't know her thinking. Perhaps she feels that internal meetings are less important than doing work that directly benefits clients. She may just have been diagnosed with lung cancer and is struggling to cope. There may be another or several other reasons. Point is: we can't know what those reasons may be until we talk openly about them.

So I might say: 'Penelope, you and I seem to have different priorities when it comes to internal meetings – can we talk about it, please?' Raising the issue from the third perspective is always the least threatening, most productive way to kick off any such conversation.

The difference between hearing and listening

Of course, one of the best ways to understand another person's perspective is to listen to them. But just because we're willing to listen doesn't mean that they will necessarily want to talk or that their motivations will be easy to grasp.

In his career as a designer, Nadim Ednan-Laperouse has created products ranging from industrial feed units for farms to

My Little Pony and Action Man play sets. He set up his first design consultancy at the age of 25 in the early 1990s. By the late 1990s, he was running a highly vaunted agency employing 14 designers.

But despite heading up an exceedingly profitable business, he felt bored. He decided that he wanted not merely to design toys for other companies but also to make them himself. Founding WOW Toys, he launched the company with five products in 1997. His brightly coloured and near-indestructible toys aimed at preschool children quickly caught the eye of retailers such as Hamleys, Toys R Us and even Tesco.

Unfortunately, the toys didn't sell. While corporate buyers loved the products, customers weren't convinced. A little digging by Ednan-Laperouse uncovered that a lot of customers were put off by the purple-coloured packaging.

Naturally, he decided to redesign the packaging, swapping the colour palette for a bright yellow. Guess what though?

'It still didn't sell. We were losing money every year. It was quite scary and we felt very out of control,' he remembers.

Desperate to learn why customers weren't buying, he arranged for 120,000 customer feedback surveys to be included in the next batch of toys. He received thousands of replies back – almost entirely from mothers – and found that many of them were eager to discuss the toys further in person.

Creating a mock toy shop and filling it with dozens of his own and competitors' playthings, he invited groups of 12 mothers at a time to chat about motherhood and toys. Observing hundreds of these mothers – up to six of these congregations a day over the course of several weeks – he learned about their complex, multi-layered mindsets.

His first discovery was that most of his buyers were first-time parents, often with the best intentions but little experience or first-hand knowledge of bringing up children. These mothers were hungry for much more information about the suitability of different toys for various age groups and to understand how particular toys might help the development of their children.

The mothers also preferred toys that provided ready-made stories. So rather than choosing a toy set comprising a plain toy car and a plastic figure of its driver, they favoured toys with names and fleshed-out backgrounds. So the Police Chase Charlie police car now comes with not only Officer Cash but also his police dog Whiskey.

Observing the mothers, he also noticed that they were drawn to certain bright colours. But their choices weren't just about whether a toy would be good for their children. Ultimately, the toys had to make the mothers feel good about themselves too.

'It's all about a mother's sense of happiness,' he explains. 'We realised that mothers could pick up toys that were wholly inappropriate for a child, sometimes even poorly made. They chose toys that were statements about their homes such as a carved lump of wood that a child would get bored of and not want to play with.'

A surprising number of the mothers chose toys that conveyed something about themselves, their tastes and sensibilities; they were choosing products that represented the lifestyles they wished to share with the world. Some were even projecting their deepest feelings and aspirations into the toys; one mother said to Ednan-Laperouse about a toy figure: 'He looks more like Marlon Brando – and more like the man I wish I'd married.'

So he discovered that he had been neglecting the mothers' needs to express themselves through their children's toys. He had initially focused only on designing robust toys with features that would keep children entertained. But with these new insights into the minds of their customers, WOW Toys completely redesigned not only the packaging but many of the toys themselves, which enabled them to turn the corner and become profitable for the first time. The company grew sales by 44 per cent last year to £5 million and currently distributes to nearly 50 countries. The five-year plan is to hit £20 million in sales to 60 countries.

'To say that our research was invaluable is an understatement,' he says.

Ednan-Laperouse's experience illustrates the clear value to be had from listening – *really* listening – to people. But listening isn't something that we're always geared up to do.

Because listening isn't just a case of asking people questions and expecting them to share their innermost thoughts and feelings, their motivations and desires. We need to make people feel eminently comfortable that we aren't going to judge them or try immediately to change their minds. We can't jump in to interrupt no matter how wrong we feel they are. To gain true insight, we must be patient and give people a totally safe environment in which to speak.

Are you a good listener? You may be thinking, 'Yes, I'm a good listener,' or 'No, I've been told that I'm a bad listener.' But thinking we're one or the other is an example of either/or rather than both/and thinking. By now you may realise that there's no such thing as a 'good' or 'bad' listener.

We can all listen when we *choose* to. Perhaps you don't listen when you're with your partner at home but you listen to your boss's boss. Or you pretend to listen when you're actually mentally rehearsing a counter-argument to what's being said. Or you sometimes follow the gist of a conversation while privately mulling over other thoughts. We all have the capacity to be good listeners when we endeavour to listen – it just takes sustained effort, concentration, and plenty of patience.

People need time to formulate their thoughts. When we decide to stop talking and wait for others to finish, we listen. When we make a conscious effort to stop glancing around the room or at a newspaper or computer monitor and focus the spotlight of our attention on another person, we listen. Silencing our inner mental chatter – the voice that allows us to wonder what we fancy for dinner – helps us to listen too.

Even when we listen, we can't expect people's thoughts and motivations to be simple or straightforward. People are complex; they can be inconsistent, contradictory, and even hypocritical at times. But the point is that we can't know what they're really thinking until we give them the opportunity to speak.

You don't need me to tell you how to listen. We all have the physical equipment we need for listening – ears, and lips that we can press together to stop us from talking. We just need to make the conscious decision to do so.

BECOME YOUR BEST: Listening as if our lives depended on it

When the stakes are high and the feelings higher, here's a great technique for encouraging people – including us – to listen. People often don't stop talking for long enough to listen and, even when they're being quiet, they're actually preparing the next argument they want to make. The beauty of this technique is that it compels both parties to listen – to *really* listen – and take on board what's been said.

Whether you're in a heated dispute with someone or you're acting as a mediator between two friends, loved ones, or colleagues, try setting an egg timer for 60 seconds or simply watching the hands of an old-fashioned clock:

1. Person A speaks for one minute while person B listens. Explain that if B interrupts, you will restart the timer.

2. Once A has finished, reset the timer. Person B then spends a minute paraphrasing what A said by using phrases like 'I hear that you ...' and 'I now appreciate that you ...'

3. Only when B has spent 60 seconds paraphrasing does B get a minute to speak about his or her point of view.

4. Finally, person A has to spend a minute paraphrasing what B said, again by using phrases such as 'I understand that ...' and 'You feel that ...'

Use this technique the next time you or any of the people around you are at loggerheads. Try it. I guarantee that you can't fail to make headway.

Onwards and upwards

Cherishing is a flair for building rapport and relationships with other people by understanding their perspectives, their thoughts and feelings. Remember that we all have the ability to cherish other people – we may just forget to use it or put enough effort into doing so. Consider the small changes you could make to have a big impact on your relationships:

- Being able to see the world from the perspective of other people, to listen to them and understand them, is a vital human skill. Find ways to remind yourself of the need to understand both the thoughts and feelings of other people.

- Be constantly on the lookout for the curse of knowledge. The more we know, the harder we find it to put ourselves into the shoes of other people, which becomes an increasing challenge for experts or people in senior roles or positions of authority.

- Research shows that even a quick reminder to consider others' thoughts can have robust benefits in our interactions with them. Find a way that works for you to ensure you switch on your 'theory of mind' ability.

- Exceptional people accept that different people can have opposing views yet still be 'right'. Focus on both/and thinking rather than an either/or choice. Look for ways to combine your viewpoints with those of others.

THREE

AUTHENTICITY

'I never went into business to make money – but I have found that, if I have fun, the money will come.'

Richard Branson

TO INSIDERS IN THE FIELDS of fashion and entertainment, Mary Greenwell is not far from being a living legend. Her current clients include actors Kate Winslet and Uma Thurman as well as Queen Rania of Jordan. Over the years, she has worked with many of the world's most famous women, including Princess Diana and Kate Moss. And I think she illustrates perfectly another capability of extraordinary people.

Meeting at notorious celebrity hangout the Groucho Club, Greenwell tells me that she had a conventional upbringing in England. She left school aged 16 because she wasn't considered clever enough by her teachers or parents for further education.

'I saw what my expectations were. It was considered completely normal that a girl should move on to work a bit, but to get married, have children, and live happily ever after,' she tells me.

She didn't know what she yearned for in life, but being a homemaker wasn't it. A year later, on a family holiday in New York, she decided that she wasn't going home. She hitched a ride across the United States to California where she worked for several years as a waitress.

'I was a lousy waitress because I used to drop plates and forget things,' Greenwell recalls.

Then, by chance, she found herself taking a job at a clothing store selling make-up. It was an unlikely choice given that, up until that moment, as a woman in her early twenties she had never even worn make-up, let alone applied it to a customer. But when she was sent for lessons to become a make-up artist, something clicked.

'As a child I was always painting and drawing. I was very, very visual. It was incredibly natural to be in this environment with brushes and people's faces,' she explains.

Only five days into her make-up course, she was asked by her tutor to make up a model for a professional photo shoot. She spent an hour with the model before nervously presenting the results to her tutor and the photographer. They loved it.

'For the first time in my life, I realised I could do something. All my life I'd been told I was stupid, that I couldn't do anything and was only capable of maybe getting married. It was such a relief to me. Wow, I can do something,' she says.

Greenwell had finally found something that made her feel alive.

'When you're starting off, you feel this challenge, this excitement. I go into this creative bubble where you lose all sense of space and time. You are so much in the present that hours can go by and you have no idea of it,' she adds.

'It's the most extraordinary thing. Everything around you disappears. It's like being in a bell jar, that's how I feel it is. It's almost like being surrounded by a duvet, in your own world where nothing else matters. Not in a selfish way but a creative way. You know the feeling will fade but for now it has that magical power,' she explains.

With such total absorption in her work, Greenwell found herself shooting to the top of her field. A not untypical day found her doing make-up in London for then-Prime Minister Margaret Thatcher before being flown to Paris to work on supermodels Linda Evangelista and Christy Turlington.

Recognition and success didn't come overnight. For years she worked on test shoots for little or no pay. But eventually she became the most highly regarded name in her field, working with big-name photographers such as Annie Leibovitz and Mario Testino. Since conquering the world of fashion, she has moved into working with Hollywood clients including Gwyneth Paltrow and Cate Blanchett, launched her own fragrance, Plum, and consulted to brands such as Estée Lauder and Chanel. For even a few hours of her time, she commands fees that top lawyers and plastic surgeons would envy.

Greenwell is quick to admit the role of timing and luck in her life. Working in a burgeoning industry obviously gave her more opportunities than competing in a shrinking one. However, I see another reason for her success. She clearly adores what she does for a living.

'It never ever, ever felt like work. It was always a game. To open up a box of toys, eyeshadows, lipsticks and blushers and then start playing with someone's face, I felt like I was ten years old. It was always new and exciting,' she concludes.

Her upbringing and schooling failed to find ways to inspire her. And it was mere chance that put a make-up brush in her hand. However, she found a profession that allowed her to come alive and, in doing so, succeed.

Feeling authentic

How do you feel on a Monday morning about the prospect of going back to work? Bursting with enthusiasm and totally fired up – or wishing it was the weekend again?

Exceptional people don't just work because they crave money. They usually work because they *love* what they're doing. 'Love' may seem like a strong word, but that's the intensity of emotion that many exceptional people feel. They genuinely enjoy their work rather than having to fake how they feel. They feel authentic.

All of the high achievers I interviewed for this book talked about the passion they had for their work. They wake in the morning full of ideas and zeal. They have fun and lose track of time when they're working. Most of them don't differentiate between work and play; for many of them, their work *is* play.

Authenticity is the ability to choose activities in life that we genuinely want to do rather than be pushed into tasks and jobs we don't like. We feel authentic when we engage in pursuits that we do simply because we find them interesting, challenging, or fun. We feel authentic when we happily do an activity without the promise of reward for doing it or punishment for not doing it.[41]

No one can be authentic 100 per cent of the time. I doubt there are many people who feel it's their life's calling to wash the dishes or take the trash out, calculate their monthly expenses or complete a tax return. We all have some tasks in life that we'd rather not do. But people who can be authentic for most or at least much of the time should not only feel better about themselves but also find success.

Hard work alone simply isn't enough to succeed. Suppose two engineers, Jonathan and Oliver, put in equally long days working for the same company. They both work twelve-hour days, five days a week.

Jonathan works because he wants to succeed. He hankers after more responsibility, the corner office, respect from his peers, and a big enough salary to buy a large house and look after his family. He doesn't hate his work, but he doesn't love it either. He finds his attention wandering occasionally, like when he's meeting with a boring customer or when he's been sent on a training course to learn about some dull new technical process. But then engineering isn't his vocation, his calling in life. He does what he thinks he needs to do to get ahead. His goals are what drive him.

Oliver couldn't be more different. He does the job because he finds it interesting, even exhilarating. He gets a kick out of meeting customers, listening to their problems, and then figuring out how he can try to help them. Of course, he'd like to earn more money so he can provide for his family. But he takes so much pleasure from his work that he tinkers around with components at weekends. He likes fixing things. He even gets told off by his wife for reading technical manuals in bed.

Let's assume that both of these people are equally bright and have similar qualifications. Who do you think would be more productive on the job? Jonathan, who watches the clock and works only because he wants the rewards of doing well in his job? Or Oliver, who genuinely enjoys his work and can't even stop thinking about it when he's supposed to be at home relaxing with his family?

Linking enjoyment and performance

Unsurprisingly, enjoyment and performance at work are tightly linked. Arnold Bakker at Erasmus University Rotterdam in the Netherlands found that professionals who said they enjoyed or were motivated by their work also received the highest job performance ratings; their colleagues were more likely to rate them highly on scales such as 'Demonstrates expertise in all job-related tasks' and 'Achieves the objectives of the job'.[42]

In a separate analysis of data on over 54,000 workers, University of Iowa researcher Timothy Judge also found a strong correlation between subjective feelings of job satisfaction and objective measures of job performance.[43] Outside of the workplace, people who report losing themselves in activities and being very absorbed in what they do testify that they are more satisfied with their overall lives too.[44]

People who enjoy their work are more productive and effective. But does feeling authentic and fulfilled in our work help us to achieve economic success? Or does the relationship work the other way around, such that people who earn more money go on to feel more satisfied with their work?

One way of looking at the issue would be to see if feelings of enjoyment and satisfaction at work at one point in time lead to bigger salary increases later. And that's precisely what investigative team Andrea Abele and Daniel Spurk at the University of Erlangen-Nuremberg in Germany did. In a rather impressive study, they sent out surveys to several thousand university students shortly after they had passed their final exams. Nothing too remarkable about that so far. But over the course of 10 years, they kept sending the participants further questionnaires every few years, asking them to answer questions about both how satisfied they were with their work and how much they earned. Over the course of a decade, the researchers gathered data on 1,336 participants who had gone on to work in professions including teaching, law, medicine, science, and the arts.

And their findings?

Participants who were more satisfied with their jobs early on experienced greater increases in salary than those who were less satisfied with their jobs. The researchers concluded that subjective satisfaction is not a by-product of objective success, but 'rather has a strong influence on objective attainments over a long time span'.[45] In other words, feeling good about our work, enjoying it and feeling satisfied by it can help us to achieve financial success too. Be happy *and* earn more. Bit of a win-win, really.

Finding pursuits that make us feel good

The more we can align our work to what makes us feel authentic, the more prosperous we will be. Some people are lucky. Serial entrepreneur Simon Hulme, for example, has known that he wanted to make and sell things for almost as long as he can remember.

'From a very young age I knew I wanted to be in business – from the age of seven I knew,' he tells me.

While most children simply lose interest in their old toys as they grow up, Hulme sold his unwanted Lego sets and toy soldiers to other kids for cash. As a teenager, he collected and sold records too, saving enough money to buy a car aged only 17.

While still at school, he then ran a mobile disco, not because he had any passion for music, but because he saw an opportunity to make money. He also tried his hand at buying and selling cars, visiting car auctions and paying for cars in cash. He made a few mistakes, losing money on more than one occasion, but nothing serious enough to dent his zeal for eking out profits from buying and selling.

Even while studying for a degree at Kingston Polytechnic – in business studies, naturally – he found a way to make a profit. He met various people who also travelled from Reigate, where he lived, to Kingston. So he offered to drive them to Kingston every day. He charged them slightly less than the bus fare, creating a classic win-win situation: they got to be chauffeured around for less than it would have cost them to travel on a crowded bus; he earned three bus fares for every car journey he made.

With such a track record, it wasn't a surprise to hear that Hulme started his first business almost immediately after graduating. At an interview for a graduate position at Cadbury-Schweppes, he got chatting to one of the other job candidates about the picture-framing business. Back in the early 1980s, framing shops typically took two to three weeks to frame a picture. But Hulme heard from his fellow candidate about a framing machine that could do the job in the course of minutes rather than weeks. The two of them decided there and then to set up a business, offering a 'while you wait' framing service.

They opened their first branch of Frame Express in 1984 and almost immediately discovered that they had more work than they could cope with. They found themselves hiring staff within a couple of weeks and opening further shops within months. Hulme later bought out his business partner and eventually sold the business for £1.75 million. At the age of only 30, he was already a millionaire. But he was just getting started.

He next spotted a gap in the market to supply quality greetings cards to small independent retailers, founding Card

Connection in 1992. Over the course of the next 15 years, he built the company up until it had sales of around £7 million a year with *profits* of over £1 million a year. He sold the business to a bigger competitor in 2007, raking in a multimillion-pound fortune.

Many people would have retired to perhaps go sailing around the world and wallow in their wealth. But Hulme is already back in business and working hard to grow a company making bespoke furniture.

'With this new business, it's fantastic. My fire has been lit again as an entrepreneur,' he says, his face and body becoming more animated as he speaks.

It's clear he isn't motivated by the money he can make. He genuinely enjoys being in business.

Hulme is fortunate – and unusual – to have known what he wanted to do in life from an early age. The majority of exceptional people I spoke to only found what ignited their passion much later in life.

Take Deirdre Bounds, for instance. Have you ever wanted to get away from it all? To quit your job and maybe flee to foreign climes? Perhaps you should do it. That's exactly what Bounds did in 1990. Fast-forward two decades and she has turned herself into a multimillionaire serial entrepreneur.

By her own admission, she had an unspectacular education. She got into university but dropped out after three years of the four-year course and took a job at a local newspaper in telephone sales.

She was barely good enough at the job not to get fired, so quit to take a marketing job at another company. Again, she didn't succeed or feel fulfilled.

She bounced into yet another job, but here got a lucky break. By chance, she met some Japanese colleagues on a training course. Mentioning that she wanted to travel, she learned that there was a massive demand in Japan for native English speakers teaching English.

Bounds quit her job and paid to complete a Teaching English as a Foreign Language (TEFL) course. She spent the next four years teaching English in Japan and China, then Australia and Greece.

On her return to the UK in 1994, though, she drifted again. She had no clear career aspirations and took a course to become a stand-up comic. For a while she wrote her own material and performed unpaid gigs in the north of England. To pay the bills, she took a job as a youth worker, supporting troubled inner-city teenagers.

'I liked the kids. They would ask me how they could start travelling like I had, but I thought there's no chance these kids could afford to travel abroad,' she says.

She felt frustrated because she had encountered many people on her travels who taught English without her TEFL qualification – many weren't even native English speakers. The world was crying out for native English speakers to teach English abroad. Unfortunately, she knew that these kids would never be able to afford the fees.

So she set up her own TEFL course, selling places on her weekend workshop for £125 rather than the £1,000 that most training bodies charged at the time. To begin with, she operated the business from her bedsit in Leeds.

'I wanted to show these kids that there was an alternative to the lives they came from. I wouldn't say I felt like a crusader, but I felt for these kids, I felt I had something to give them,' Bounds adds.

For the first time in her life, she felt excited about a project. Far from dreading the prospect of turning up to work in the mornings, she found a reason to work hard. Her company quickly expanded across the UK. By 2007, her training and travel company i-to-i was operating in 35 countries and certifying 17,000 TEFL teachers a year.

She sold the business to travel giant First Choice for an eight-figure sum – upwards of £10 million. After taking more than a year out to think about her options, she has stepped back into the entrepreneurial ring with Parties Around the World, an online venture to engage young children with charitable giving. The company only launched in 2009 but the early signs are that it will grow quickly and raise a lot of money for good causes.

Bounds only succeeded when she found something to ignite her interest, her motivation. At school and in the early years of her career, she could easily have been labelled by people as a drifter or career failure. She became fired up about work only when she found something that had meaning for her. Her passion came from wanting, really wanting, to give inner-city kids a chance to broaden their horizons and escape the squalor of their home situations. Getting rich was a happy coincidence.

Even her decision to sell i-to-i was based on her desire to play to her strengths rather than cash out and make money. Once the business got to a certain size, she realised her limitations as a manager and chose to return to her entrepreneurial roots.

Bounds found what switched her on, what made her want to jump out of the bed in the mornings. Over and over, I meet business moguls, philanthropists, sportspeople, entertainers, and managers in large organisations who say that they love what they do. Ordinary people seem capable of achieving extraordinary feats when they find their way into situations that suit them. Do you know what suits you?

OVER TO YOU

Finding what gets us fired up may take a bit of trial and error. People like i-to-i's Deirdre Bounds and make-up supremo Mary Greenwell stumbled on to their sources of motivation. You might never discover that you're a born scuba-diver, ski instructor, or alternative health therapist until you try. Perhaps you have a stellar talent for sculpture, an amazing facility with words and language, or a knack with computers. But you might never find out unless you give it a shot.

The implication? Seek out more, diverse experiences. Try your hand at different stuff. The activities that may allow us to feel authentic might be things we've never considered. So get into the habit of broadening your horizons by trying new experiences. Who knows, you may suddenly find your calling. Practise saying 'yes' to new experiences and seeing where it takes you.

BECOME YOUR BEST: Taking stock of your work

Too many people put up with the drudgery of their jobs because it pays the bills – but that's hardly the attitude that high achievers adopt. If you desire to succeed, you must do work you enjoy. Otherwise you will only ever be a fraction as effective as you could be. To begin the process of moving your career on a better trajectory, work through the following questions:

● In what kinds of work situations have you worked harder than you normally do?

- What have been the highlights of your working life? Why?

- What activities do you pursue in your free time when you have no other obligations? Why?

- If you could do different activities on separate days of the week, how would you structure your time?

Take your time in auditing how you spend your time. Write down your thoughts. Perhaps scribble a few initial ideas, then refine your answers over the course of several days or even weeks. The more deeply you think about what makes you tick, the better your chances of shaping your career and life into something you not only relish but can succeed at.

Spotting experiences of 'flow'

I can't overstate the importance of finding work that feels like play. Losing track of time while we're doing an activity is often a good sign that we're being authentic, that we're engaged in something we genuinely enjoy.

One way to identify what feels authentic is to look out for experiences of what psychologists call 'flow' – moments in which we're so immersed in what we're doing that we don't notice what else is going on around us.[46] Hours slip by and feel like minutes. We can't ruminate about the past or worry about the future.

Athletes describe such moments as being 'in the zone', often when they train or compete. They are so focused that they can't feel sad or angry or tired. They don't even feel happy. Because to experience any emotion – even a positive one – would take their focus from the activity they're performing. It may only be afterwards that they think, 'Wow, I was really in the zone.'

Only then are they flooded with glee or gratitude for the intensity of the experience.

At its core, flow is about being engrossed, totally absorbed in a task rather than merely having fun. It's like being in a tunnel, seeing only the task at hand. Research shows that when we experience flow, our self-belief blossoms and we improve at what we're doing.[47]

When we have an experience of flow, we may:

- Feel in control

- Experience a sense of challenge

- Lose track of time

- Feel fully involved

- Want to tell other people about it

Can you think of occasions when you've felt at least some of those sentiments? This next exercise is a different way in which you may be able to discover what helps you to feel authentic.

BECOME YOUR BEST: Identifying your high points

Think back over the course of your life and bring to mind at least 10 occasions when you felt lost in what you were doing. Be sure to consider all areas of your life. This isn't just about your work. You can go as far back in time as you like – some of these episodes may have occurred when you were a child while others may even have occurred in recent months.

Write down a few sentences about each. Put each experience on a separate sheet of paper. Then, for each peak experience, consider:

- What skills was I using?

- Who was I with?

- What were the circumstances? *What made the experience special?*

No one else has to see your list, your thoughts. This exercise is for your benefit alone so dig deep and avoid limiting yourself only to activities that other people might consider impressive.

Once you've got your list of 10 experiences – or more, remember – take a look at the themes. What kinds of skills crop up most often? What are the implications for what you should be doing, how you should be spending your time?

But here's the killer question. How many of your peak experiences happened in your current job? If *none* – not a single one – of your 10 high points has been in your current job, why are you doing it?

One of my early peak experiences was when I worked at logistics and transport company Federal Express – many years before the company rebranded and became simply FedEx. While at university, I took a summer job as a data entry clerk, entering address and package details into a computer system. So here are my answers to the three questions from the box above.

- What skills was I using? I enjoyed it partly because I liked (and still like) working with computers. The software programme wasn't that easy to use so I had the occasional opportunity to help reboot the PCs – I learned a lot about computers that year. And I was a fast, accurate typist so I could do the job well. I felt good at my job.

- Who was I with? Nearly two decades on, I can still remember Karen ('Kags') and Zita, the two supervisors who were endlessly chatty and fun to be with. Plus there was a whole gang of other students and young people who all seemed to be at a similar stage of life to me.

- What were the circumstances? *What made the experience special?* I was working with a young, fun team. No one was trying to climb the career ladder. No one was engaged in politicking or backstabbing. Our work wasn't all-consuming so we could chat and joke while we worked. It taught me that I like to be part of a fairly small team in which everybody knows each other really well.

I coach many people who are so busy doing their current jobs that they've lost track of their end goals; they know they're not entirely happy but are too tired, too frazzled to consider what else they could do. Taking stock of our lives occasionally can be really beneficial. Revisiting our past, our jobs, interests, and activities can allow us to see patterns and make better career and life decisions in the future.

Another example: from an early age, I used to put on plays and give monologues to my (very tolerant) parents, aunts and uncles, and family friends. I lost that confidence in my teenage years. But I rediscovered it in adulthood. Now I get perhaps the biggest buzz from running seminars or speaking to vast audiences of many hundreds of people at a time. Educating a throng of managers about leadership or peak performance is fun for me. Standing on a stage and speaking to a crowd of entrepreneurs or employees is often the highlight of my week.

Maybe you used to play an instrument in an orchestra or were on the committee of an amateur theatrical troupe. Perhaps you enjoyed writing an essay, a report, or press releases, and haven't done so for years. Or you really enjoyed a project in which you had to interview dozens of colleagues or customers. When we dig deep to recall when we were at our peak, we can identify how we might live our lives to be both satisfied and successful.

Finding the intersection of interest and talent

Understanding the pursuits that challenge or excite us is a great start. But enjoying an activity isn't enough to guarantee results.

When I said earlier in this chapter that Authenticity is the ability to find activities that we find rewarding, that was only half of the story. Exceptional people don't just do what they enjoy – *they also do what they're good at.*

Often, what we enjoy and what we're good at are one and the same. When we enjoy something, we spend more time doing it. So we get better at it. But that's not always the case. Sometimes we may not have a natural talent. And being authentic is at least partly to do with identifying when we should give up. Because too many people try to pursue lives or careers for which they're really not suited.

Watch the early rounds of TV talent shows such as *The X Factor* or *American Idol*. You'll see people who want to make it as singers who can't sing a note. The same goes for reality shows like *Big Brother*. I've acted as a commentator on the show for years and have seen many contestants declare that they want to pursue careers as TV presenters or actors, even though it's clear to the world that they lack the raw talent to make it.

High achievers understand what they're good at and find ways to play to their strengths. Some people are naturally better at numbers than others, or better at speaking in public, working with their hands, planning and orchestrating, inspiring people, repairing machines, and so on. Having a natural knack for something doesn't mean we can sit back and relax – we still have to nurture our talents in a sustained fashion through practice, coaching, feedback, and more practice. And of course we can all improve on just about any dexterity with determination and practice. But in most cases we're better off finding pursuits in life that allow us to exercise our natural talents than fighting an uphill battle to develop skills that don't come easily.

OVER TO YOU

Here are a handful of sentence stems. Use them to jot down your thoughts on your favourite skills, your strengths, your natural talents. Feel free to use each sentence stem as many times as you like. Aim for as many completed sentences as you can, then see how much overlap there is between what you're good at and what you currently do at work on a daily basis. This will help you to think about what you currently do and what you could perhaps be doing differently.

- People have often said that I am good at . . .

- Close friends value me for . . .

- I can always be relied upon to . . .

- Colleagues come to me because . . .

- I often find myself offering to . . .

Taking alternative perspectives on talent

How easy do you find it to identify your talents? Not everyone finds it straightforward to recognise their natural talents.

The problem often starts early in our lives. Schools tend to promote a fairly narrow definition of aptitude, which is predominately focused on the ability to learn and regurgitate information. So a lot of people grow up thinking that they have no skills – that they're stupid or untalented.

Thankfully, psychologists increasingly acknowledge that there are in fact many different ways in which we may be talented or intelligent. Howard Gardner, a professor of education at Harvard University, has received wide acclaim for proposing eight eclectic talents that we may all possess to varying degrees:[48]

- Verbal-linguistic talent – including skills in reading, writing, and communicating through words. Playwrights, journalists, orators, and even people in public relations excel in the linguistic arena.

- Logical-mathematical talent – an aptitude for performing calculations, analysing puzzles, deducing patterns and rules in data, and solving logical problems.

- Visual-spatial talent – being able to picture objects and manipulate them mentally. For example, people who are strong at this tend to have a good sense of space and direction.

- Bodily-kinaesthetic talent – having finesse with our bodies and hands. Think of surgeons, sculptors, builders, or dancers who rely on being physically coordinated.

- Musical talent – aptitudes to do with rhythm, music, and hearing. Individuals who are strong in this area may play instruments, sing, or compose.

- Interpersonal talent – being sensitive to other people's moods and motivations; understanding relationships and being able to build relationships easily.

- Intrapersonal talent – sometimes called emotional intelligence, this is a flair for understanding our own thoughts, emotions, and motivations. Many of the exercises in this chapter are aimed at developing our self-awareness, our intrapersonal talent.

- Naturalistic talent – a flair for working with the natural world, including not only animals and plants but also their natural surroundings.

Do any of those non-traditional talents resonate with you? The point is that human talent and capability are diverse and multi-faceted. Traditional education focuses on a restricted definition of intelligence – almost exclusively on verbal-linguistic and logical-mathematical talents. But I'm sure you can appreciate that people can pursue brilliantly successful careers and lives in myriad ways.

If, for example, you have an aptitude for building things, repairing equipment, and using your hands, you may find that the typical office job may be a somewhat limiting path to take in life. Or if you have a naturalistic talent, perhaps a role that allows you to get out of the office and into a literal field may be a better way not only to feel authentic but also to succeed. Whatever your strengths, be sure not to take them for granted.

Shaping a satisfying and successful career

No matter how little or how much you enjoy what you do, you can find ways to relish it more. True, more than a few people see their work as something to be endured. They live for their evenings and weekends and resign themselves to being either unhappy or only moderately happy at work. But people with the capability of Authenticity don't always find themselves in work they love, so sometimes they have to work on the *nature* of what they do.

Harvey Mayhew is managing director of the UK division of a public relations firm. When I first met him nine months ago at a corporate dinner, he made an off-hand comment about not particularly enjoying his work. He spent all of his time in internal meetings, managing financial, human resources, and IT issues. He was proud of the growth he had created in the business but at the same time wasn't entirely enthused by the prospect of his job any more.

I asked him when he had felt happiest, at his peak. I could almost see him gazing into the past. He described occasions when he'd been pitching to clients, standing in front of them and choosing the right words to win their business.

I questioned why he couldn't do some pitching again. He said it 'isn't the way it's done'. As managing director, he was supposed to entrust pitches to his account directors and their teams. To step in and get involved would imply that he didn't trust them, that he was meddling.

We left it there initially. But when I met Mayhew a couple of months later at his office, a spacious office with floor-to-ceiling windows and a view of the river Thames, I pushed him on how he could adjust the nature of his job.

Eventually he decided to offer his three account directors more of his responsibilities. He put it to them that, by getting them involved in more of the internal human resources, IT, financial, and operational issues, he was preparing them to step up to his level, to be a potential managing director. He encouraged one account director to take charge of staff recruitment, another to get more heavily involved in working with the finance director, and the third to work with the European IT and facilities teams to oversee the firm's technology and facilities. By freeing up around a day and a half of his time every week, Mayhew was able to do more of what he enjoyed most. He persuaded his account directors that he could help them to approach further and bigger clients in a bid to win more business.

If you discover that you aren't doing enjoyable activities and using your favourite skills much in your current job, one option is to quit and find more fulfilling work elsewhere. An alternative is to tweak your role to enjoy it more. Rather than accepting passively that our jobs will always be the same, we can find ways both to feel more fulfilled and to achieve more.

Researcher Amy Wrzesniewski at the Yale School of Management has spent most of a decade examining the relationships between what people do at work and how satisfied they feel. She identified that some people manage to engage in something she calls 'job crafting', redesigning their own jobs in ways to make them feel more fulfilled.[49] She found that job crafters help themselves to feel more satisfied with their work, even in jobs that at first seem to have very rigid duties attached to them – jobs such as cook, cleaner, and assembly-line worker. Having studied many occupations in a variety of organisations, she noticed that job crafters use one or more of three different tactics to sculpt out their jobs:

- **Altering the boundaries of the task** by taking on more tasks or expanding the scope of tasks that they enjoy. For example, an employee who enjoys fixing broken-down equipment could offer to do it for colleagues. By approaching line managers and colleagues, nearly everybody has the opportunity to fine-tune how much time they spend on favourite tasks.

- **Modifying their relationships at work,** to alter the nature or amount of their interactions with other people. For instance, an employee could choose to spend more time with certain customers, suppliers, or even colleagues to get more enjoyment out of the job. An employee could perhaps volunteer to train colleagues on new ways of working, present updates to senior managers, seek feedback from clients, or handle customer complaints, negotiate better deals with suppliers, and so on.

- **Changing their perception of their work,** by reframing the work, thinking of the bigger picture, or consciously making an effort to imbue the work with a sense of purpose. For example, a hospital cleaner could see the work as a means to help ill people rather than simply cleaning. An insurance administrator at a call centre could think about the job as a way to take the hassle out of callers' lives. A hairdresser could think of the work as a competition, seeing who can cut the most hair in a day, or perhaps a social service, making customers feel better about themselves.

One way of looking at job crafting is to think of our jobs as a series of flexible building blocks. We can move the building blocks. By saying, 'I'd like to do that,' and volunteering for particular projects or pieces of work, we can bring in new building blocks. And by working more efficiently or by partnering up with colleagues, we may be able to hand off or delegate other building blocks too. By reshaping the nature of our work, we can help ourselves to not only relish the work more, but be more productive too.

BECOME YOUR BEST: Crafting the perfect career

What proportion of your job do you enjoy? Want to enjoy more of it?

The exercises in this chapter so far have asked you to look back on your career; they will have given you a good idea about the kind of tasks you most enjoy. But you may benefit from looking forwards too.

Keep a diary and reflect briefly at the end of every day on the best moments you had. Take stock over the course of several weeks to identify which pursuits you enjoy the most. What do you enjoy doing, when, where, and with whom?

If you like to see things visually, plot the ways you spend your time on a graph. The vertical axis measures how much you enjoy activities. The sideways axis measures how important the activity is, how much it's valued perhaps by colleagues, bosses, or customers.

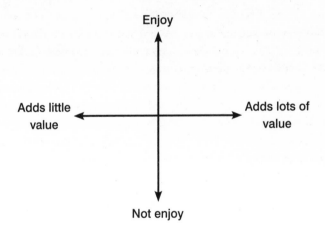

Then you can start modifying how you spend your time, gradually pursuing more positive/high-value moments (activities that fall into the top right quadrant of the graph) and reducing the time you spend doing the less enjoyable/low-value pursuits (activities that fall into the bottom left area) with a view to eliminating them entirely.

The further you break down how you spend your time into its constituent parts, the better the result you'll get. For example, a client who works in finance began his list as follows:

- Giving instructions to my personal assistant

- Getting instruction from the senior partner

- Writing agendas for the day's meetings

- Holding one-to-one meetings with members of my team

- Holding client meetings

- Writing slide presentations

- Checking over the spreadsheets that my junior analysts have put together

Say you're currently spending only 10 per cent of your time with clients. You'd like that proportion to be more like 40 or 50 per cent. Maybe you could ask colleagues if you could shadow them occasionally. Go along to one more client meeting a week – or even just one more a month if that's all you can manage at first. Then, once you've proved your value, see if you can bump that up to a few more every week or month.

I'm not saying that it'll be an overnight transformation. Savvy job crafters take a strategic outlook, adjusting a few elements of their work at a time, over the course of months. The point is that we can take action, take control, rather than merely putting up with a job. We can find ways to feel more fulfilled without necessarily moving to new pastures.

When we help ourselves to enjoy what we do, we feel more motivated and may get noticed for all the right reasons. Indeed, research shows that the more employees take control of their jobs, the more valued they are by their line managers.[50]

So do you want to be both more productive *and* more highly regarded?

Onwards and upwards

Authenticity is the ability to choose activities in life that we genuinely want to do. We feel authentic when we engage in pursuits that we find interesting, challenging, or fun. Bear in mind that even small adjustments to how you spend your time could reap significant benefits:

- Consider the extent to which you can say that you genuinely feel engaged and alive at work. Research shows that people who enjoy their work are far more likely to earn more than people who are simply putting up with their work.

- Think back to high points both in your career and outside of it. Piece together a picture of the skills you most like to use. The more you can bring your favourite skills into your work, the more engaged and effective you will become.

- Take stock of what you're good at too. Finding activities you enjoy isn't in itself enough to succeed. Remember that exceptional people pursue activities that they relish and have a natural talent for.

- Take a strategic approach in crafting the perfect job. Volunteer for the tasks and activities you enjoy; aim to spend more time with the colleagues, customers, and other people you treasure most. Changing the shape of your career will take time but can be very rewarding – both emotionally and financially.

FOUR

CENTREDNESS

'The cyclone derives its powers from a calm centre.
So does a person.'

Norman Vincent Peale

James Averdieck is managing director and a founder of Gü Puddings, the purveyor of upmarket chocolate desserts. The 53 per cent cocoa-solid desserts arrive not in cheap plastic containers but elegant glass ramekins that are aimed strictly at grown-ups with indulgence in mind.

Averdieck launched the company in 2003 with a chocolate soufflé that, when heated gently in the oven at home, treated consumers to a hot chocolate sponge crust filled with molten chocolate lava. Since then, he has launched dozens of other products and has started selling the products on the Continent, to the notoriously fickle French too. He estimates that a Gü pudding is eaten somewhere in the world every two seconds, which helped the company to make £26 million in 2009. Yet there's still more to come.

'In five years' time, my vision is to get to £100 million and to be a brand that is well known throughout the Western world,' he tells me.

Most entrepreneurs would sell their parents into slavery to create such a popular and lucrative brand. After all, he beat off competition from multinational companies such as Cadbury and Müller. Yet I get the distinct impression that he doesn't quite recognise the scale of his achievement. I ask him to identify the turning points in his journey, the difficulties that he experienced along the way. He shrugs, saying that he hasn't really experienced any difficulties or setbacks. He says that his success comes down to hard work and a healthy dose of luck. But I'm not satisfied with his answer so I push further.

I come back to the question later, asking him to tell me about the transformative moments in his career. Towards the end of the interview, I pose the question in yet another way by asking him about his darkest moments. He takes a long pause to think. Yet he still can't recall any.

Of course Averdieck isn't saying that there haven't been challenging times in his career. At the very beginning of his journey, he worked with a chef to fashion the right recipe for a restaurant-quality pudding. However, he had considerable problems turning out an artisanal product in the industrial quantities he needed. He ended up throwing away large amounts of it, which could have been quite dispiriting, especially as it was his own money, his own dreams that he was almost literally flushing down the drain.

On his office wall, Averdieck also has a large framed photograph of Gü ice cream, a reminder of a product that he launched in 2005. It failed to dent the market and was dropped. Lesser people could easily moan about these events but he is pragmatic and almost emotionless about these episodes.

But I realise that he's not emotionless. He demonstrates a sense of humour and unabashed enthusiasm for his work. He is excited about the prospect of continuing to grow the business over the coming years. He talks about the thrill of the chase and the buzz he gets from every aspect of his work. He clearly experiences positive emotions – he's just blissfully free of the negative ones. He seems able to brush off the worries and occasional bouts of frustration or despair that touch most other people. He has the gift of Centredness, a sense of inner calm, collectedness, and self-assurance that allows him to withstand any knock.

The inner world of the exceptional person

Some people seem to possess bucketloads of confidence. Whether they're with a single person or a thousand, they're not afraid to speak up. They tell gripping or amusing stories, laugh easily, and become the life and soul of most gatherings. But how people behave when they're in public is only half the story. We often assume that people who appear confident must surely have an inner sense of self-assurance too. That's not always the case though.

Truly exceptional people possess another quality, a different skill. They possess Centredness, an ability to manage their inner mental life, moods, and emotions. They aren't insulated from failure; instead they find the mental strength to pick themselves up when they get knocked down. Rather than struggle on under the weight of roiling emotions, they find ways to work through them and recover. In doing so, they allow themselves to sustain high levels of motivation and performance even in the face of adversity and the most crushing of defeats.

Many of the exceptional people I've interviewed – including pudding king Averdieck – don't even realise they possess the skill of Centredness. Most people focus on the outward behaviours of what they do and say rather than the inward processes of how they think and feel. Because Centredness is an inner expertise, the workings of which are invisible to onlookers, people who possess it can at times appear fairly unassuming. They may appear reserved, quietly spoken, unadventurous, or even shy. Their outward demeanour may reveal nothing of the steely mental toughness within.

Vicious words and compassionate comments

What are you thinking right now? Stop reading for a moment to think about what you ate for breakfast and you'll 'hear' the sound of your thoughts in your head.

That voice is what psychologists call our inner speech.[51]

Sometimes we may have flashes of inspiration or ask ourselves hypothetical questions. But more often our stream of consciousness is a rather dull mix of reminders and casual observations such as 'I must catch that train at half past,' and 'Oh, it's raining again.'

Listen for long enough and we may hear our voice congratulating us at one moment and chastising us the next. Our voice may build us up with comments like 'This is going really well,' and then bring us down only moments later with 'Oh no, I'm so stupid!' and 'I knew I shouldn't have done that.'

Psychologists have known for decades that how centred we feel depends on the ratio of negative to positive thoughts we tell ourselves.[52] The more negative messages we hear, the worse we feel. If we allow ourselves to dwell on fears, regrets, and worries, we feel down, less centred, less able to think clearly and get on with life.

Now our feelings can be uncomfortable territory for many people. At work, for example, we're encouraged to get on with the task, to brush off our feelings, and do whatever we need to. But simply ignoring how we feel has the potential to cripple our effectiveness in just about every area of our lives.

For example, say you're a manager looking to fill a vacancy. All other things being equal, wouldn't you rather hire someone who brushes off setbacks than one who suffers from more extended mood swings? Or if you were a customer looking to buy an insurance policy, wouldn't you rather deal with the cheery salesperson than the one grumbling about whatever is bothering them?

Of course the answer to both questions is 'yes'. And research tells us that happy, centred people are more likely to receive a second interview than their less happy peers.[53] Salespeople with a positive, centred disposition also sell more than their more downbeat counterparts.[54]

Our feelings bleed out and affect those around us – a phenomenon that psychologists call 'emotional contagion'. For example, when the leader of a team is either happy or angry, that sentiment can influence the mood of team members. Unsurprisingly, leaders who display positive rather than negative moods are rated more highly by their teams.[55] And leaders who remain upbeat when their teams are under pressure help the teams to perform more effectively than leaders who allow themselves to get angry.[56]

Seminal studies – including one investigation that tracked the careers of 13,000 people over 16 years – even show that people who are happy and centred go on to earn considerably more than gloomier people.[57] Happy, centred people have more prosperous marriages, a better quality of life; they live longer too.[58]

Whatever our definition of success – whether that's earning power, relationship satisfaction, or physical health – it seems that being centred can help us to achieve it. Happiness doesn't necessarily come from being successful. Research tells us that being centred *causes* success.

OVER TO YOU

Even supremely well-centred people tell themselves off or worry occasionally. A good starting point to becoming more centred is to dissect how you tend to think and what triggers your patterns of thinking.

Would you say that your thoughts are mostly positive or negative? Given that Centredness is a key component of high achievement, to what extent do you need to dampen down negative thoughts and encourage more positive ones?

Nurturing our natures

Some people seem naturally gifted with an unshakeable sense of self-belief and collectedness. Such individuals may be born with more of a tendency to listen to their supportive inner voices. Others may naturally hear their destructive voices more. But can we really choose to tune in to the helpful voice rather than the critical one? Can we really improve our mental resilience?

Research shows that between 20 and 40 per cent of our likelihood of suffering from conditions such as depression may be down to our genes.[59] That may sound like a big chunk of our fates that is determined by the random combinations of our DNA.

But let's talk about your physical health for a moment. We know that coronary heart disease has a strong genetic component, that certain genes passed down from parents and forebears can multiply our chance of having a heart attack.

Say one person, let's call him Jack, smokes 40 cigarettes a day and drinks a bottle of wine on his own most nights. He works long hours and can't be bothered to eat breakfast or lunch. His favourite dinner is something like an Indian takeaway followed by a handful of doughnuts. Unsurprisingly, he's very overweight – his doctor tells him that he is clinically obese.

Jill, on the other hand, doesn't smoke. She only drinks the occasional glass of red wine at weekends. She works long hours too but starts the day with oatmeal porridge with a banana chopped into it. She watches her weight by eating a salad or small portion of pasta at lunchtime and perhaps a piece of fish with vegetables for dinner.

Out of Jack and Jill, who would you bet on to get to the finish line?

Regardless of our family's medical history, we can either guarantee ourselves an early demise or help ourselves to live long and healthy lives. The make-up of our DNA doesn't tell the whole story. And the same goes for our resilience, our Centredness, our ability to withstand psychological shocks and setbacks.

Or let me put it another way for you. If your boss said that 20 to 40 per cent of your end-of-year bonus would be determined by factors outside of your control, that still means that 60 to 80 per cent of it will be based on your efforts, on what you can do. You'd be pretty happy with that, wouldn't you?

Our genes and early upbringing may influence our patterns of thinking and feeling in certain ways, leading us to be naturally more cheery or gloomy in our outlook on life. But those ways are not set in stone. Respected scientists such as the University of California at Riverside's Sonya Lyubomirsky have gathered an impressive body of studies showing that, no matter how optimistic or pessimistic we tend to be, we can use tried and tested techniques to boost our psychological hardiness, our ability to centre ourselves.[60] Decades of psychological science and research into psychotherapeutic techniques tell us we can help ourselves to feel less anxious, less unhappy, less angry, and more centred simply by *choosing* to change how we think.[61]

Focusing our attention on the here and now

One of the most profound lessons I've learned as a psychologist is that thoughts are just thoughts. No matter how troubling, terrifying, or distressing our thoughts, they are not reality. Agonising over something that happened in the past doesn't make it any better. Worrying about something that might happen doesn't make it any less likely to happen.

The pattern I've noticed in my research on exceptional people is that they focus their thoughts strongly on the present, on what they're doing at any given moment. They don't let their minds wander back to past blunders. They don't fret over what could or might transpire. They focus intently on the present, not the past nor the future.

We can all decide what we pay attention to. When misgivings or worries pop into our heads, we could give them the full weight of our attention and mull them over, replaying past regrets or pondering predictions about the future. We could worry about what we should or shouldn't have done. Or fret over what might happen when we have a critically important meeting or a big date the next day. The more helpful alternative, though, is to choose to let such thoughts pass and focus our attention instead on what we're doing and what's going on around us right now.

Our attention is like a spotlight that we can shine on whatever we like. Try directing your attention to your breathing, on the rise and fall of your chest and the sound of the breath entering and exiting your lungs. Then focus on the events going on around you. Perhaps there are people nearby or you could home in on what's going on outside your window, a splodge of dirt on a wall, or anything else around you.

You can turn your attention inwardly too, if you like. When you're in a conversation or meeting, you can allow your attention to drift away from what's being said. You can concentrate instead on your inner speech, your thoughts, the list of groceries you want to pick up on the way home or the joke you heard the other day. Or dwell on painful past events or something you're dreading in the future.

Mindfulness is the tendency to focus on what is going on around us in the present moment. Being mindful means directing our attention to what's going on around us rather than the thoughts we have in our heads. In direct contrast to being absent-minded or mindlessly going through the motions, it's about savouring what we're doing rather than being mentally miles away.

I originally trained as a sport and exercise psychologist before moving into executive coaching. Last year, I worked with a professional football player who earns in a couple of weeks what most people earn in a year. I can't say much about him because football fans are notorious for their attention to detail, their ability to remember the tiniest facts and hints of trivia, and I don't want to give his identity away. When we met for coaching, he was so keen to hide his identity that he even paid cash for my help.

His main issue was that he often had troublesome thoughts flashing through his mind during football matches. Even in the middle of a game, he worried about the consequences of missing a crucial shot, passing the ball to the wrong person, making a bad decision. Over the course of a year, we worked together on helping him to become more mindful during games, on focusing his attention outwardly on the game itself – the ball, his teammates, the opposition – rather than his mental observations and worries. And it's paid dividends. He says that he feels both more relaxed and more focused. He can concentrate fully on the game rather than on what *might* happen or *could* go wrong. He's playing better too.

Research investigations have discovered that people who are naturally more mindful tend to be more centred, more satisfied and successful. Several studies show that being mindful helps us to stay centred when others around us are distressed.[62] Romantic couples who are naturally mindful reported greater satisfaction with their relationships than less mindful couples.[63] Another study found that, amongst MBA students, mindfulness was associated with better exam performance too.[64]

The good news is that we can train ourselves to be more mindful when we need to be. Mindfulness training over the course of only eight weeks has been found to help romantic couples to feel more emotionally connected.[65] Mindfulness training has also been shown to be a powerful method for treating psychological conditions ranging from chronic depression to eating disorders. [66]

BECOME YOUR BEST: Attending to the world mindfully

The concept of mindfulness is derived from the Eastern practice of meditation. But far from being a mysterious art involving bells and chanting, modern mindfulness training is scientifically proven to deliver results. Becoming mindful is essentially about training the spotlight of our attention to focus outwardly on our situations, what we're doing and the people we're with rather than inwardly on our own thoughts. Try to become more mindful in everyday situations and you will begin to see the benefits when you need it most.

When you're having a conversation, focus the spotlight of your attention on the other person or people – avoid letting your attention drift inwardly. When you're eating a meal, try to focus on the tastes, the textures, the smells so you can really appreciate the food. Or when you're lying in bed at night, clear your mind and focus simply on the sensation of your breathing, feeling your belly button rising and falling with each breath. The same goes for just about any situation or activity, whether that's driving a car, exercising, listening to a lecture, watching a movie, even making love.

When distracting or unhelpful thoughts pop into your head – and it happens to everyone – imagine that they are small boats floating by on a river. Use your imagination to zoom out from the scene and give yourself a bird's eye view of the landscape below. Visualise allowing your thoughts to recede into the distance. You can observe them passing by without overanalysing them. And then, without beating yourself up for the fact that your thoughts wandered, simply bring your attention back to whatever activity you're doing.

Try threading mindfulness into your daily activities – even the mundane ones. Doing so will give you the best shot of detaching your rational mind from your sometimes irrational thoughts when you're under fire. Then, when you do feel overwhelmed, you may be able to distance yourself from your thoughts, allowing you to see matters in perspective. The more you practise mindfulness, the more you can enhance your Centredness, your ability to restore your composure.

Becoming more mindful takes practice. Most people find that they can only manage to be mindful for a few minutes at a time to begin with. And no one can be mindful all of the time. But, with perseverance, they find that it helps to stave off unwanted thoughts, helps them to enjoy what they're doing, and enables them to become more centred, more productive.

Feeling better FASTER

Focusing the spotlight of our attention outwardly on what we're doing is increasingly viewed by psychologists as one of the best ways to stay centred. But sometimes we may have too many thoughts roiling around in our heads for us to shake them off. When we've been brought low by a persistent, niggling set of negative thoughts, we may need to find another way to fight them off.

The FASTER technique is an example of what psychologists call a thought record, a proven method for combating negative thoughts and becoming more centred.[67] The more we get into the habit of quizzing our illogical thoughts, the more proficient we can become in keeping negative emotions at bay and staying centred.

BECOME YOUR BEST: Challenging negative thoughts

When you feel in an emotional funk, don't let your thoughts fester. Take an interlude to grab pen and paper to work through the six steps of the FASTER technique to confront your thoughts and emotions instead:

1. **Feelings.** Write down the unhelpful instincts, the tumultuous emotions you're experiencing. Rather than using broad and overused terms such as 'unhappy' or 'depressed', try to be as specific as you can, for example writing that you're 'disappointed', 'resentful', 'tense', and so on. Also give each emotion a rating from 1 to 10, based on how strongly you feel each one.

2. **Actions.** Jot down how your feelings might be affecting your behaviour in unhelpful ways. What would you like to be doing? Or what would you like to stop doing? You might be avoiding going on a date or quitting your job, for example. Or you may be drinking too much alcohol or taking your anger out on a loved one.

3. **Situation.** Next, describe briefly what happened to trigger those feelings. What were you doing? Who were you with? Did someone do or say something – or was it certain thoughts or mental images that triggered these unhelpful feelings?

4. **Thoughts.** Write down the unhelpful thoughts that are running around in your head. Perhaps you're worried: 'I'm going to get fired,' or 'They don't love me any more.' Capture all of these thoughts so that you can help yourself to see through them.

5. **Evidence against your negative beliefs.** Time to look for ways to contradict your unhelpful thoughts. First of all, what's the name of your most supportive friend? Now imagine him or her asking you questions such as: 'Is that *really* true?' or 'What's a better way of looking at that?' Look for the flaws in your negative thoughts; demolish them and you help yourself to escape from their grip.

6. **Review feelings again.** Finally, re-evaluate your feelings. Looking back at the feelings you wrote down in Step 1, how strongly do you now feel those emotions? By working through these six steps, you should feel less emotional, more centred.

Exceptional people seem to keep unhelpful thoughts away without even realising it. For many people, though, practice is needed to make it become second nature. The more familiar you become with using the technique, the more you will get out of it.

Aim also to use the technique as quickly after a challenging event as possible. You may not always be able to use the FASTER technique when you're in the clutch of negative thoughts and feelings. Perhaps you're in a meeting with colleagues or have other matters to attend to first. Even if you must wait until the end of the day to reflect on a particular situation, you will still get the benefit because you are gradually training your mind to correct the way you think and feel about the world.

Expressing our emotions

When problems or difficulties strike, it's natural to feel angry, sad, ashamed, bitter, and so on. On a day-to-day basis, being more mindful and challenging our destructive thoughts using the FASTER technique can help us to stay centred and productive.

Occasionally, though, certain major events can leave us feeling totally devastated – losing a job, a bout of ill-health, the loss of a loved one, or having a massive row with a close friend. When such episodes happen, we could end up feeling down – and less productive, less motivated, and even less creative – for not just hours or a few days but weeks or even months. Time to wheel out the more powerful techniques.

I work with Birgit Du Preez, a forty-something tax adviser. She originally came to me for guidance after a major setback. Nearly 10 years ago, she and two business partners had set up an accountancy firm. They grew the business very smoothly for six years. When the growth began to slow, she and her partners decided to merge with a larger accountancy practice for financial security. Last year, when the merger was finalised, her partners decided to oust her from the firm. Not because she was performing poorly in any way but purely because they could make more money without her there.

Du Preez was devastated. Both of her original partners had sided with the owners of the new firm to push her out. She had seen them as close friends. Much worse than simply being fired from a job, she felt betrayed. She felt violated to have been driven out of the business she had built.

When we first met, several months had passed since she had been ejected from the business. However, I quickly realised that she wasn't ready to think about next steps in her career. She needed to wrap up past events, to deal with the emotional turmoil that was still roiling within her, before she could move forward. So I encouraged her to write about her experience, to describe not only what had transpired but what she had felt.

Du Preez was sceptical. She was a finance expert, someone more used to dealing with numbers than feelings. A little grudgingly, she agreed to give it a go. When we next met, she raved about how much she had got out of writing about recent events and the sense of loss and grief she had been feeling. She showed me the pages and pages of notes she had typed up. She had found it so cathartic, a massive release of the frustrations and feelings that she hadn't quite realised she had still been bottling up.

We've all heard that it's bad to repress our feelings and emotions. One research study found that people who were instructed to push negative thoughts and emotions out of their minds actually became more rather than less distressed.[68] So we should never try to block off our instincts when we feel badly let down by a friend, upset by a loved one, or angry over a work situation.

Our feelings are messages from ourselves – internal memos – with a warning or meaning to impart. An emotion such as anger may point to actions to take or changes to make in our lives such as 'I need to speak up about this issue,' or 'This isn't the right situation for me in the long term.' Sadness may tell us 'I need my friends around me right now.' Even fear may tell us 'This is a major challenge and I need to do much more preparation for it.'

The rights and wrongs of emotional expression

Negative emotions can be like a toxin. They can continue to circulate around our systems, poisoning our minds, making us sluggish and ineffective until we drain ourselves of them. Thankfully we can accelerate our recovery by embracing our emotions. However, simply getting the emotions out into the open may not be enough.

One team of scientists looked at three different methods of exorcising the negative emotions associated with traumatic life events. Participants were subjected to a battery of tests measuring not only psychological but also physical health. They were then randomly assigned to write, talk into a tape recorder, or think privately about a bad experience they had been through. They were all requested to spend 15 minutes each during three consecutive days writing, talking, or thinking about their experiences.

Four weeks later, the individuals who had either written about their experiences or recorded them on tape reported not only enhanced mental health but also better physical health compared to the group who had only thought about their experiences. In fact, the participants who only replayed their experiences mentally actually reported *worse* well-being and health.[69]

Not everyone feels comfortable talking about their experiences and recording them. But we all have access to pen and paper or a computer to write about the negative experiences we've been through. Before you get started, though, let's consider a pair of studies that tell us how to get the most out of the technique.

Psychological researchers Ethan Kross and Ozlem Ayduk looked at the impact of giving different instructions to participants as they recalled negative life events. Participants were randomly assigned to one of two experimental groups. One group was urged to immerse themselves in the negative episode – 'to relive the situation as if it were happening to you all over again'. The second group was prompted to replay the experience but to do so from the point of view of an observer – 'watch the experience unfold as if it were happening all over again to the distant you'. Seven days later, the participants who had recalled the event with a distanced perspective reported feeling significantly more positive than those who had been instructed to immerse themselves in the negative experience.[70]

BECOME YOUR BEST: Getting the most out of emotional writing

Expressive writing can be a powerful technique for dealing with the emotional fallout of intensely negative situations. Aim to repeat the technique by writing on each of three consecutive days.

Bring to mind a significant experience you'd like to recover from. Your goal is to write about your deepest thoughts and feelings regarding the episode or situation. In your writing, really let go and explore your deepest emotions and thoughts. You may wish to think about how it affects your relationships with people such as significant others, parents, friends, or relatives. You may wish to refer to your past, present, or future – to who you have been, who you are now, or who you would like to be. Don't worry about spelling, grammar, or sentence structure. Just write.

Based on research examining what makes for expressive writing, here are three important guidelines to follow:

- **Go back to the episode, but take a few steps back and move away from your experience.** Watch the experience unfold as if you were watching it from the point of view of an outside observer.

- **Write about the meaning of the event and its implications rather than simply describing it again.** Even tragic circumstances may have hidden positive consequences. Try to recast the event to uncover any insights or lessons rather than merely replaying painful memories.

- **Remember to look back on your situation with compassion.** You would naturally express concern to a friend who had gone through a gruelling situation. Make sure to express understanding and kindness for yourself too.[72]

Ideally, you would write for between 15 to 30 minutes on each of the three consecutive days. But even as little as two minutes is better than nothing.[73]

Psychology researcher James Pennebaker is widely recognised as a guru on the psychological benefits of writing about harrowing experiences. Analysing the essays that 177 participants had written, he discovered that certain words were linked to greater improvements. In particular, words to do with insight (e.g. 'realise', 'see', 'understand') and words to do with causation (e.g. 'because', 'infer', 'thus') were most strongly associated with benefits. People who merely described the situation (e.g. 'did', 'felt', 'believed') or reported how they felt at the time (e.g. 'angry', 'sad', 'joyful') reported fewer benefits.[71]

Several studies have looked at the benefits of expressive writing. Students who used the technique found that their grades improved. Unemployed middle-aged engineers who wrote about the experience of being out of work found new jobs more quickly than those who didn't. And, in some studies, participants who used the technique also reported that they felt physically healthier – they even paid fewer visits to their doctors.

Remembering to unwind in appropriate ways

I once met Andy Bond from supermarket giant Asda. We were both about to be interviewed on the same BBC television programme and when he introduced himself and said that he was 'in charge' of Asda, I assumed that he meant he ran one of their stores. My mistake: he was actually the chief executive, running *all* of the stores in the country.

When I did some digging about him afterwards, I discovered that he likes to keep fit. In an interview with *The Times* newspaper, he said: 'I used to be a competitive sportsman, doing athletics and rugby. Now I run, I cycle, I go to the gym. My only real extravagances in life are posh trainers and a posh racing bike.'

He's not alone in taking fitness seriously. Many of the exceptional people I've worked with or known are sporty too. And, working with the recruitment team of a large professional services firm, I discovered that they decide which candidates to bring in for interview based on various characteristics. Having a top degree from a good university gets you one point. Speaking an additional language gets you another point. Competing in a physical activity or team sport gets you another point too. Physical fitness and high performance seem to go together.

It makes sense when we think about it. *Mens sana in corpore sano*. A healthy mind in a healthy body. A high-performing mind in a fit, high-performance body.

So how do you like to spend your leisure time? Occasionally, we may feel the need to switch off. After a bad day, there's nothing wrong with relaxing, taking a soak in the tub, chatting with a close friend, or having a sing-along to your favourite tune. But, unlike many other forms of recreation, physical exercise may actually help to recharge our mental batteries.

Research tells us that exercisers report greater levels of psychological well-being than non-exercisers.[74] And several research trials suggest that moderate physical exercise may be as effective as talking therapies and even certain drugs in the treatment of clinical depression.[75,76] It may be a particularly potent method for remaining centred because it both distracts us from our worries and floods our bodies with endorphins, our natural feel-good hormones.[77]

In experimental trials that a colleague and I conducted at the University of London's Institute of Psychiatry, we examined the mood-boosting effects of light physical exercise. We measured participants' mood before randomly assigning them to either light physical exercise or an equivalent period of quiet relaxation. Measuring their mood afterwards, we discovered that even the single session of exercise quelled negative emotions such as anxiety and anger while enhancing positive emotions such as elation and excitement. In addition, the single bout of exercise had stronger mood-boosting effects than mere relaxation.[78] I really do urge you to go get those trainers out of the cupboard and get your heart rate pumping.

OVER TO YOU

Even if you can only manage to engage in some form of physical exercise for 10 or 15 minutes a day, you help to reset your stress reactivity. Never think of yourself as being 'too busy' to take a brisk walk. Sure, many people manage to work exceedingly long hours for extended stretches of time, but the human brain is after all housed in a flesh-and-blood body that needs tuning and care to operate at peak effectiveness. Think of exercise as an invaluable investment in your continuing effectiveness in everything you do.

Be careful of being drawn into leisure activities that actually drain rather than refuel us though. I like to watch escapist TV dramas late at night. Even when my favourite show is over, I'm occasionally tempted to keep the TV on, to surf channels. When I do so, I find that time has passed, but that's about all that's happened. Do I feel more educated or inspired, rested or invigorated? No. None of the above.

John Robinson, a social scientist at the University of Maryland, looked at survey data asking 45,000 Americans about their habits and levels of happiness. Comparing happy versus unhappy people, he was unable to find any differences in their education, the number of hours they spent at work, or even how much they earned. His one standout finding was that unhappy people watched 30 per cent more TV every day than very happy people.[79] A similar study in Europe of over 42,000 people in 22 countries found that people who watch more television not only feel more anxious but are also more materialistic too[80] – a finding that makes sense, as advertisers would certainly hope that watching television (and their adverts) makes people more eager to buy their products.

Don't get me wrong. I'm not knocking television. As a psychologist, I've helped television producers to make a fair number of TV shows. And good television can be as magical and moving as any form of art. But television in large doses is like a drug that can anaesthetise rather than replenish us, making us feel *less* rather than *more* centred.

Many activities are enjoyable and beneficial when consumed in small doses. We all need time to unwind, to flick through a trashy magazine or stare at the TV for a while, to surf the Internet, enjoy an unhealthy snack, and so on. But more is not always better. We can have too much of a good thing. The occasional scoop of ice cream may be good for the soul; a glass of red wine may be good for the heart. But three scoops of ice cream a night is a guaranteed route to obesity; three glasses of wine every evening a sure-fire cause of liver damage.

OVER TO YOU

When we stop to take stock of how we spend our time, we usually know when we are living our lives in ways that help us to stay centred. To help you stay in peak psychological condition and allow you to perform consistently at your best, are there any activities you should be doing *less*?

Onwards and upwards

Centredness is the ability to maintain our emotional equilibrium in the face of adversity. Remember that it's a dexterity that we can all develop and not just a gift only certain people are born with. Consider that even modest tweaks in how you think about yourself and the world could deliver hefty benefits:

- Aim to become more mindful. Make a conscious effort to focus your attention outwardly on what you do every day. High achievers rarely dwell on their internal thoughts, worrying about the past or fretting about the future.

- Be sure to challenge the negative messages that your mind may tell you. Galvanise your more positive self to look for more positive ways of looking at situations as if you had a sympathetic friend supporting you.

- Avoid suppressing troubling emotions. When you want to move on from a bad situation, try writing about it. Emphasise the implications, lessons, and insights so you can process those experiences and move on.

- Unsurprisingly, mental resilience seems to go hand in hand with physical health and fitness. Think about how you could reduce certain activities to make time for even a little physical exercise in your schedule.

FIVE

CONNECTING

'When we seek for connection, we restore the world to wholeness. Our seemingly separate lives become meaningful as we discover how truly necessary we are to each other.'

Margaret Wheatley

SUPPOSE YOU HAVE A BRILLIANT business idea. You know you could make millions from it. To launch your idea, you need to gather the managing directors, finance directors, and marketing directors from a dozen of the largest companies in the country under one roof. But you have no budget for marketing or a big publicity splash. What do you do?

Rob Farbrother was in that exact situation in 1995. At the time, he was chief executive of the Link cash machine network and in recent months had noticed utility companies putting electronic terminals into shops. He tells me that his first thought was: 'What the heck did they do that for? There's something weird here.'

Puzzled, he did some digging and discovered that regional electricity companies were beginning to put terminals into supermarkets and other retailers to collect cash payments from customers. He discovered that, despite the availability of payment options using telephone banking or electronic transfer, a vast number of customers were still paying with cash. Many of them didn't even have bank accounts. And because the Post Office was charging the utility companies up to a whopping £1 every time a customer paid a bill at one of their counters, the utility companies were being forced to buy expensive terminals to collect cash payments – like cash machines in reverse – in a bid to reduce their running costs. The thing is: each of the individual utility companies was paying for its own network of terminals. To cover a town or city, each electricity company would have to provide a terminal, each water company would have to provide a terminal, and the gas company a third terminal. Looking into the future, Farbrother spotted that there would be a lot of unnecessary overlap.

So the idea for a business popped into his head: 'Hang on, why don't we get all of the electricity companies together, all of the water companies together, and British Gas, and they can share an infrastructure?'

But getting in front of some of the country's most influential executives wasn't going to be easy. Farbrother knew he had a good idea – even a great one – but it was still only an idea. It would cost a lot of money to research the project, to do a feasibility study. And he didn't have access to the head honchos.

His solution?

He approached the people he knew, asking them for advice. In particular, he found his way to one contact, a partner at the accountancy firm Price Waterhouse (now PWC).

'I said, "I've got a problem. Do you know these people? Can you help me? Because if I asked them to turn up to a presentation in London, they don't yet know who Rob Farbrother is, and no one's going to turn up. But I need the finance directors, the managing directors, the marketing directors from every organisation."'

His contact agreed to host the event, using the Price Waterhouse brand name and pulling power to attract the senior executives from all of the utility firms. It was a classic win-win situation. The partner at Price Waterhouse positioned himself and his firm to help the utility companies in evolving their internal systems should the project achieve lift-off. And of course Farbrother won too.

'That started it off. That got the interest. I got the contacts. We followed up the presentation with a survey saying, "Are you interested in taking this further? Would you pay £30,000 to investigate this further?" And so we got people interested enough to put money on the table to take the research further,' he explains.

Farbrother was on his way. He created the PayPoint brand in 1996 and launched it to the public a year later with an initial network of around 1,000 terminals offering facilities where customers could pay their household bills.

Today there are some 22,000 PayPoints in the UK and Ireland and Farbrother is a multimillionaire. After his triumph with PayPoint, he decided to repeat his achievement in Continental Europe. He set up PayShop, a similar business in Portugal, which he sold for around 11 million euros. His current venture is in the arena of estate agency – and who would bet against him succeeding yet again?

His success in developing PayPoint hinged upon the critical moment when he needed to get in front of the big utility companies. He didn't have connections to the people he needed, so he exploited his network, the personal relationships, the connections he had. It's a lesson that exceptional people in any field learn very quickly: no man or woman is an island. The most savvy, successful people draw on the support and strength of their friends, contacts, and acquaintances; they recognise that people collaborating together get better results than individuals struggling alone.

When I explain the principle of using our connections to individuals I'm coaching, they often say: 'But I don't know anyone *important*!' Good news, though: you don't have to.

Ask and you shall receive

As the 1990s gave way to the twenty-first century, Carmel McConnell had it all. She was running her own corporate consultancy for clients including 20th Century Fox, UBS, and Whirlpool. She only worked three days a week but still managed to pay herself a six-figure salary. And she was in a happy long-term relationship with her partner.

'I was living a fairly comfortable, if hard-working life,' she tells me.

She was researching to write a book on social activism and had a big question in mind: 'Have we created a fairer as well as a richer society?' Friends told her to start by interviewing school head teachers in a fairly deprived part of London. She was shocked to discover that around one in four children were arriving at school often too hungry to learn.

McConnell was stunned.

'I had a nice home in a nice part of town. I had a very happy home life. I had no material needs. I'd become one of those "them" that doesn't really know what's going on,' she recalls.

'The teachers said: "The reality is we have toasters here in the classrooms because the kids haven't had anything to eat since the free lunch they had the day before." I was shocked, so shocked. And I thought, for all the success that I've had, I can't believe there's a Dickensian situation going on around the edges of the city,' she says.

She responded by dropping off healthy breakfast food to five schools as part of her regular weekly shop. But after a year of doing that and running her business, she realised she wasn't making enough of a difference. She tried to lobby government on the issues of child poverty in the UK, but gained little headway.

'I thought, right, I need to think about this. I took a loan out on my house, gave myself two years' salary and just thought, "I have to go for this and solve this problem."'

And so began Magic Breakfast, the charity that McConnell started in 2001. By the end of 2009, the charity was feeding 2,500 children at 62 schools. The plan is to be serving 10,000 children at 250 schools by the end of 2010.

Surprisingly, though, she tells me that Magic Breakfast has no full-time paid members of staff. Neither is the charity funded by the government nor donations from the public. So how has she managed to afford enough food to feed thousands of mouths every day? And how does she manage the sheer logistical challenge of getting food to dozens of schools at locations dotted all over the capital?

'The ethos is that we can use the leverage of our partners,' she says.

And by that, McConnell means that she reaches out. She picks up the telephone. She writes letters and emails. Rather than waiting for people to offer their assistance, she goes to them.

'I met someone at a dinner party who said she knew someone who worked at an investment bank and I said, "Do you mind if I write you an email telling you what we do, because I'd love to work with you to make a difference in these schools." She forwarded it on and my email wound up on the desk of the head of community engagement who was looking for a food-related programme and the next thing we knew, we're in a beauty parade with six other charities. We got through and received £50,000, enough money to support 25 new schools,' she says.

It's an example of the power of networking. Even though we may not know anyone important directly, we may know people who know the right people.

Another time, she was watching a television programme about

the billionaire founder of one of Europe's highest-profile financial firms. She got in touch immediately.

'I wrote to him and said: "You're one of the richest men in London. If you're interested in supporting kids so they can achieve their potential at school, then I'd love to have a chat."'

Next thing she knew, she received a call from someone at the financier's charitable foundation. Within days, she had a donation to buy food for the 45 schools that she was supporting at the time.

McConnell joins boards and committees too, continuing to grow her address book of contacts and finding her way to big brands such as Quaker Oats and Tropicana fruit juices, both of which agreed to partner with Magic Breakfast. The charity also recently celebrated having supplied one million breakfasts to children who would otherwise have gone hungry.

McConnell succeeds because of her willingness to approach people. Rather than waiting for her charity to be noticed, she goes to them. Forthright and ambitious for the children she seeks to feed, she makes no apologies for broadcasting her intentions and asking for help.

Connecting the dots

In totally different fields, Rob Farbrother and Carmel McConnell reached out. They recognised that they could work to best effect with other people. And in just about any walk of life, we can all be better, stronger, more effective if we seek to collaborate rather than soldier on alone.

Creativity, for example, comes from many sources. Sure, we could sit in a room trying to dream up beautiful new ideas. But really, we need stimulation. And how better to be inspired than by meeting fresh faces in divergent fields and seeing the world through others' eyes?

If you're an entrepreneur with an idea for a revolutionary new product, you may still need to find investors who will sit up and notice. Or say you're a singer, an actor, a would-be TV presenter. Even if you're great at what you do, you still need to find a record label, a Hollywood studio, a TV channel to give you your shot.

The same goes for professionals in most walks of life. If you're an accountant or surveyor, consultant or designer, you must find a way for customers or clients to pick you out from the crowd of your rivals. Or if you work within a large organisation, you need your bosses to recognise your talents if you want to get those sexy projects and promotions too.

It's no use simply getting on with what you do in the *hope* of being discovered. Hope is not a strategy. Why not make yourself heard and help people realise who you are and what you can do?

We all know the old adage that getting ahead isn't about what you know, but who you know. Some cynics take the saying as evidence of the unfairness of the world. But researchers simply acknowledge the reality that connections help us to secure more opportunities. Monica Forret at St Ambrose University refers to 'what you know' as human capital and 'who you know' as social capital. She argues that: 'Social capital is more difficult to imitate than our human capital. Similar education, training and experiences are much easier to obtain and replicate than our relationships with others. Who we know, and the quality of our relationships with individuals is a unique, valuable, non-replicable asset.'[81]

So I say that getting ahead is about what you know *and* who you know. Just as your intellect and expertise are a source of talent, so is your ability to build and maintain relationships.

High achievers don't complain about the fact that opportunities – breakthrough ideas, business leads, career openings, and even money to start businesses or support charitable causes – go to those who are well connected. They see their connections as an asset that they can expand and capitalise on. They take action by making new connections and finding ways to maintain old ones.

Connecting is the skill of reaching out to people, building relationships, and staying at the forefront of their minds. There are probably people out there who have common values, similar goals – but they can only help us and work with us if we make contact and stay in touch with them. They can't rally round if they don't know we exist.

Putting the work into networks

Gavin Ellwood has a unique perspective on the art of Connecting. Like many people running their own businesses, he spends a lot of time meeting people at formal and informal work gatherings, trying to forge new relationships, and ultimately generating leads for his company. But as one of the founders and owners of fast-growing executive search firm Ellwood & Atfield, he also sees the other side of Connecting – from the viewpoint of organisations and the senior people who make hiring decisions.

'Networking is vital if you want to advance, progress, learn, create and exploit opportunity. If you're not interested in those things – and that's not a judgement – then networking isn't vital. It's only important if you want to achieve certain things, and I see those things as being success and advancement,' he tells me.

I can't imagine there are many people around who aren't interested in success and advancement of either the personal or professional kind. Ellwood argues that all professionals – ranging from engineers and dentists to architects and alternative therapists – should raise their own profiles and introduce themselves to more people. Why?

'Most people who wear a suit don't make something, so there isn't an object that can speak for itself. There isn't a sample of your work that people can pick up and study for its quality, craftsmanship or beauty, its value. So the only thing that does exist is you.'

Ellwood believes that we all need to introduce ourselves to people and let them know what we can do, what we can offer. Otherwise, how will they know to come to us when they – or the people they know – happen to need someone to provide the kind of service that we provide?

But few people feel comfortable with the notion of networking, of wandering around at a conference or forced social gathering. Is it perhaps a knack that only naturally extroverted, outgoing types can excel at?

'I'm actually not very sociable, but professionally I'm gregarious because I understand that it helps me to be successful,' Ellwood confesses.

'I'm not particularly interested in chatting to folks at parties or finding out about them. I have my circle of friends, my family, and I'm rather happy with that, thank you very much. But at work, I can be more successful by being professionally gregarious and speaking, engaging with more people, and engaging with large groups. So it's not my default position, but I've learned to do it.'

Psychologists agree with his point too. While some people are naturally more extroverted, we can all cultivate the finesse of social connectedness.

'People will say, "I'm not naturally sociable," or "I don't like a big roomful of people, I don't feel comfortable talking to people in that way." I don't feel comfortable doing certain aspects of my job. I don't enjoy writing, but I have to write reports, that's part of my job that I don't enjoy but I have to do it. And networking is no different to that. It's just part of your job. And it's not something that the vast majority of people are not able to do. They just choose not to,' Ellwood adds.

Networking is a skill that, like any other, can be honed through practice. However, effective networking is not about talking incessantly about yourself and shoving your story down people's throats. Of course we must all be willing to answer questions about ourselves, what we do and why we do it. But bragging is clearly repulsive. No one is saying that we need to push ourselves in other people's faces. Accomplished networking is more about asking questions, listening to the answers, and looking for ways to help rather than be helped.

The key is finding what interests other people and looking to find the overlap between what we have and what they want. Often, we may have little in common with the people we meet; but research tells us that networking may occasionally present us with the right person to help us with a big charitable donation,[82] a new job offer,[83] or whatever else we may need.

BECOME YOUR BEST: Uncovering your connections

Whatever your occupation, trade, or role in life, you can become more effective by understanding your connections. Perhaps you're a teacher, manager, writer, administrator, secretary, charity worker, or parent. You'd be surprised at the number of associations and groups that encompass the different roles you have.

The following questions are from a ground-breaking piece of research. Answer the questions for now and I'll get to the point afterwards. Here's a single question to begin with. How often have you attended meetings of business-related organisations? Use the following six-point rating scale to rate your attendance:

1 = never

2 = seldom, only once or twice a year

3 = occasionally, several times a year

4 = moderately often, every few weeks

5 = often, almost every week

6 = very often, almost every day

Here are some further questions. There's a different rating scale, so please note that this scale differs from the previous one:

1 = zero times

2 = one time

3 = two to three times

4 = four to five times

5 = six to seven times

6 = eight or more times

WITHIN THE LAST YEAR, HOW OFTEN HAVE YOU . . .	SCORE
Given professional seminars or workshops?	
Accepted speaking engagements?	
Acted as a commentator for a newspaper, magazine, or talk show?	

Published articles in a company newsletter, professional journals, or trade publications?	
Taught a course?	
Attended professional seminars or workshops?	
Attended conferences or trade shows?	

Now, add up the scores you got for all eight questions (not only the seven questions in the table but also the question at the top of this section). You should have a score of between 0 and 48. Researcher Monica Forret established that people who got a higher score by engaging in a greater diversity and frequency of professional activities tended to earn more than people who didn't.[84] A score of less than 10 puts you in the bottom 15 per cent of people, while a score of 20 or more would put you in the top 15 per cent.

So how well did you do? However you scored, the rest of this chapter will give you practical guidance on how to boost not only the quantity but also the quality of the connections you have.

Not everyone is comfortable with the traditional idea of networking, of attending trade shows or cocktail parties and foisting themselves on lots of strangers. But Connecting is much broader than mere networking. Notice that many of the questions in the quiz above point to other ways to engage with people such as writing articles for industry publications.

Think too about volunteering to sit on committees, boards, and even judging panels for industry or departmental awards. The point is simply to meet more people in whatever ways you feel comfortable. Whether your goals are to do with philanthropy or personal advancement, social activism or empire building, consider how you could build your coterie of supporters and take what you do to the next level.

Seeking the spark

As you can imagine, the people I interviewed for this book had busy schedules. They juggle board meetings, important clients, international travel, requests from journalists – and try to fit them around their family and social lives too. So it took many phone calls and emails to find convenient times and places to meet many of the people who graciously gave me their time.

A friend once told me that his mantra in life is to 'go where the energy is'. And I like to say that I 'seek the spark' when it comes to Connecting to new people. When you meet people, see if there's some kind of spark, some kind of energy or genuine connection between the two of you.

If there's little or no interest, then by all means give it another go. And another. And perhaps another. But if you've put your case to someone more than a handful of times and there's still absolutely no interest, it may be sensible to seek out other people, other avenues. Because there are people out there who *want* to connect with us. Better to put our efforts into finding them and nurturing those relationships than pestering people who may at best develop only a grudging relationship with us.

BECOME YOUR BEST: Pursuing genuine connections

More than a few people associate networking with schmoozing at conferences or other public events, being fake and pushing business cards at people. Thankfully, that's *not* Connecting.

By all means go and meet new people. Chat and ask a few broad questions about what they do and what they're interested in, and listen to their stories. But if you have nothing in common with them, leave it at that. If you don't like them, don't fake it. If you're not genuinely

---

interested in what they have to say, nod along politely until the conversation naturally comes to an end. Keep their contact details until a time when you could get back in touch with a genuinely good reason. But don't pretend to be anything that you're not.

Keeping in touch with people purely because you think they might be useful to you smacks of manipulation. You will feel uncomfortable; and because people are so innately sensitised to falseness and faked friendliness, they'll feel used. You both lose.

Better to stay in touch only with people you admire or genuinely want to talk to, learn from, or help. If you find each other funny or entertaining, that's good reason to stay in touch, to perhaps meet again for social reasons. If you think you can contribute to their goals, again, let them know; perhaps write them a note afterwards expressing your admiration and a specific way in which you could help. Or maybe you could introduce them to other people *you* know who could benefit from meeting them.

Wildly successful people blur the lines between work and play. As most high achievers love what they do, they don't feel the need to separate their work associates from their personal buddies. Rather than trying to develop more business contacts, aim to be a sincere, proactive, helpful friend to a few more people. Perhaps that's by weaving yourself into your community or workplace or making a bit more effort with your friends and friends of friends. Think net*friending*, not networking.

Helping people invokes the universal norm of reciprocity; enabling others to achieve their goals makes them feel more inclined to return the favour. Chances are that genuine friends will be more inclined to come to you or recommend you than the business acquaintances you may contrive to create. So look for ways to have fun with people or help them out and you may find yourself building a surprisingly sturdy coalition of people who are not only friends but supporters.

Reminding people that you exist

Whatever the methods you choose, Connecting comes down to the same thing. It's about meeting more people and letting them know what you can do that will help you both to succeed.

The research is clear on this too. Hans-George Wolff at the University of Erlangen followed up an assortment of several hundred employees over a three-year period. He found that people who networked not only enjoyed far larger increases in salary but were also more satisfied with their jobs than people who didn't.[85]

So if you want both to earn more *and* enjoy your work more, perhaps it's time to start Connecting a little more. Ramp it up, take it to the next level.

If you work within an organisation (as opposed to running your own business), you could do worse than to learn from Mike Hodges, a senior banker at financial titan HSBC. He currently works as head of international and new business at HSBC's Corporate Banking Centre in London, looking after multinational client organisations with sales of over $250 million. When I met him five years ago, he had received rave reviews from both his peers and bosses as part of an evaluation exercise that I was conducting with the bank. And I read about him in the press over the summer for having won various banking prizes, having edged out competitors from banks including Lloyds TSB.

In a bank with tens of thousands of managers and employees, Hodges has risen quickly. Yet he didn't join a graduate fast-track programme; in fact, he joined what was then Midland Bank before it was acquired by HSBC, straight from school with few qualifications. His first job was in a high street branch sorting bank statements. How did he do it?

'My strategy when I joined was to get as high up as I possibly could as quickly as I possibly could,' he tells me.

His first role was as a junior clerk. His second job within the bank was as a cashier. Both jobs were in sleepy towns in the west of England. He needed a way to improve his prospects.

'If you were trying to get on in the bank at that point, you needed somehow to go through the regional head office where the regional director was sitting and somehow build your internal profile. If you worked in his team and he's looking through a list of people to appoint and sees you on his list – it became apparent to me that going through this regional head office was not a bad place to work,' he explains.

Working in a branch, he occasionally had reason to call the credit and risk department within the regional office. So he asked to spend time shadowing that team to understand more about what they did. Impressed by his willingness to learn, they were more than happy to oblige, letting him spend two days with them. A month later, he was invited to take a job in the regional head office. He spent 18 months there and was swiftly promoted first into junior and then middle management.

'I think I was probably the youngest of that grade in the bank at that time. I would have been 26 years old. It's about making your own luck, making your own destiny, not waiting for opportunities to come along,' Hodges argues.

He moved away from the regional head office and back into the branch network. But when the bank restructured and created a Southern Division with a regional head office just south of London in Crawley, he again realised that he needed to make himself known.

'I had to find a way of increasing my internal network, increasing my PR coverage. If you'd asked the guy in Crawley who headed up the division if he knew Mike Hodges, the answer would have been "no". So I wanted to work in that team so that the man at the top and all those senior people who didn't know Mike Hodges branch manager would know Mike Hodges,' he says.

Again, by making the right career move and being noticed, he vaulted further up the bank's hierarchy, becoming a senior manager within the bank along with the not-insubstantial pay and pensions package that goes along with it.

To me, his actions exemplify what can be achieved when a person thinks strategically and makes the right connections; Hodges realised that senior people can only reward us if they know about us. He has similar advice for people further down the hierarchy too.

'If someone in the bank picked up the phone and said to me, "I'm hearing some good things about corporate banking. Can I come and spend a few days looking at what you're doing?" I'd respond quite positively to someone making the effort. Then if we advertise a role and you've got six applicants and one of them has gone to the trouble of seeing what the team does and got to know us as individuals, I think generally you're more likely to pick somebody who wants the role. We try to pick people here who really want to do it,' he says.

It sounds so obvious when Hodges tells me his story and his viewpoint on the simple steps people should take to help themselves in their careers. But so few people actually *do it*.

BECOME YOUR BEST: Improving your internal visibility

If you work within an organisation, this next set of questions – again from research – will be of particular interest to you. Use the six-point rating scale below to say how much of each activity you've done.

1 = never

2 = seldom, only once or twice a year

3 = occasionally, several times a year

4 = moderately often, every few weeks

5 = often, almost every week

6 = very often, almost every day

WITHIN THE LAST YEAR, HOW OFTEN HAVE YOU . . .	SCORE
Stopped by others' offices to say hello?	
Gone to lunch with your current boss?	

For the next set of questions, please note that the rating scale differs:

1 = zero times

2 = one time

3 = two to three times

4 = four to five times

5 = six to seven times

6 = eight or more times

WITHIN THE LAST YEAR, HOW OFTEN HAVE YOU . . .	SCORE
Accepted new, highly visible work assignments?	
Been on highly visible task forces or committees at work?	

Add up your scores for the four questions to get a total of between 0 and 24. Again, researcher Monica Forret found that people who scored highly on quizzes measuring their internal visibility tended to earn more than people who tended to ignore such activities.[86] A score of 17 or more puts you in the top 15 per cent of people; a score of 9 or less puts you in the bottom 15 per cent.

How does your score stack up? Remember that even senior people are only human. They are busy and have their own concerns, so sometimes we need to remind them about our talents and achievements. This isn't about talking yourself up and pushing your agenda in any sinister way. This is simply about having a regular dialogue with senior people, volunteering to work on projects that both benefit the organisation and get you noticed, and reminding people at all levels of the organisation that you're there to help. So what do you reckon you could do more?

Maintaining the right connections

I work as a business psychologist, coaching executives and entrepreneurs on how to be better leaders – more effective, more confident, more accomplished and successful. And I used to avoid hanging around with other business psychologists. Why let them in on my trade secrets?

But my reading of the research tells me that my logic is flawed. In fact, my thinking wasn't just a little wide of the mark, but totally incorrect. Because there's mounting evidence that the people we surround ourselves with can have a profound effect on the kind of people we become.

Analysing data based on hundreds of thousands of Danish citizens, Stanford University researcher Jesper Sørenson found that people who worked alongside former entrepreneurs were more likely to start their own businesses.[87] Of course that makes sense. Meeting people who are ex-moguls may plant the idea of entrepreneurship. Such associations may also help to transmit valuable lessons that give people the confidence to strike out on their own.

Our health may be affected by the kinds of people we meet and socialise with too. Harvard University professor Nicholas Christakis found that people's risk of becoming clinically obese was significantly related to their social ties. In an analysis of data gathered from 12,067 people over the course of 32 years, he found that a person's likelihood of becoming obese escalated by 57 per cent if he or she had a friend who became obese.[88]

No surprises there either. If you have a friend who's heavily overweight, he or she is hardly going to slate you if you put on a few pounds. Even if that criticism might actually help you to become healthier, it's unlikely to come from your clinically obese friend.

Other studies have similarly found that the likelihood of turning to crime is significantly elevated when individuals have friends – or even friends of friends – who are criminals.[89] So it's just as our parents have always suspected. Hanging around with the 'bad kids' from school really can lead to delinquency and even a criminal record.

Both ideas and social norms creep from one friend or associate to the next. Our beliefs about what is either desirable or taboo are shaped by the people we know, with profound implications for the people we should surround ourselves with.

We need to find like-minded people if we're to reach our goals. If your goals are to be an entrepreneur or author or entertainer, you need to mingle with business founders or writers or other would-be entertainers. If your goal is to climb the career ladder or move into a different industry, you need to make sure you're meeting the right senior folks. Or if your goal is to quit smoking or become a better parent, be sure to find your way to non-smokers and other parents too. And for a business psychologist like me, I need to spend more time with other business psychologists who can spur me on to greater heights.

Widening our circles

We all have different social and professional circles. Take your friends, for instance. You probably have a small cluster of people you'd consider to be your closest, your best friends – folks you confide in and trust totally. Then you have a slightly larger group of people you consider to be good friends. Perhaps you don't see them as often or you don't share as much of yourself with them. And then there's probably an even larger circle of friends that you might almost consider acquaintances: you enjoy their company when you meet up, but you don't see them or even speak to them terribly often.

The same goes for your professional contacts. You probably have a small posse of colleagues, customers, and business associates that you see regularly. Then there are some you see less. And others you hardly see at all.

When I coach people – whether they're entrepreneurs running their own businesses or managers within a larger organisation – I almost always find that they could use their circles of friends, contacts, and acquaintances more effectively. Whatever their goals, they can usually benefit from Connecting more.

So I tell people to draw up a list of their contacts, the people they know. Next, I ask them to rate the strength of their relationship, perhaps by giving each person between one and three stars, depending on how well you mutually know and like each other. Here's an example:

NAME	STRENGTH OF RELATIONSHIP
Andrea Briers	*
Oliver Holden	***
Hing-Chee Tang	***
Jennifer Stalk	*
Eddie Rangaswami	***
Martin Horowitz	**

Now, say you have a particular goal – perhaps to raise money for charity, promote your business or find a new job. You may be tempted to stick to the safe ground of getting back in touch with the people who know you best – your three-star and two-star relationships. But research tells us that may not be the most lucrative course of action.

As far back as the early 1970s, sociologist Mark Granovetter suggested that our so-called weak ties – the people we know least well – may be disproportionately important when it comes to achieving our goals.[90] Because the people we know best tend to be highly connected to each other. Looking at the table above, for example, it's likely that Oliver Holden, Hing-Chee Tang and Eddie Rangaswami are most likely to know each other already. They may have worked in the same companies or similar industries; they may have overlapping circles of friends too. If we had met with Holden, then it's likely that we would learn more from meeting one of our other contacts rather than Tang and Rangaswami.

Our weak ties may act as bridge-builders between communities. For example, say a person – let's call him Darren – works at a law firm. Many of his best buddies and contacts will also tend to be male lawyers or people in similar fields such as banking and accountancy. But having a woman friend or contact who works as a fashion designer allows Darren to tap into whole new communities of fashionistas who may need a lawyer or know other acquaintances who could do with a lawyer too.

Several studies highlight the power of weak ties. One investigation surveyed employees and managers in three very different organisations: an American pharmaceutical company, a British bank, and a Canadian oil and gas company. The research team led by Daniel Levin of Rutgers University found that while most people relied on their strong ties for knowledge and advice, the most useful information often came from the weak ties rather than the people they were in contact with most frequently.[91] Another study found that job seekers who made the additional effort to connect with their weak ties tended to earn more in their next jobs than their counterparts who focused mainly on the people they already knew well.[92]

Belonging to a greater number of social factions and networks may even help to protect us from illness. More than a few studies show that people who have more diversified social networks live longer than people with fewer types of social relationships.[93] Most remarkably, the relative risk of death for individuals with few social networks is comparable in magnitude to the impact that cigarette smoking has on mortality.[94] Putting it another way, having few friends is as dangerous for our health as taking up smoking.

Perhaps rather puzzlingly, though, people with more friends don't necessarily have better health than people with fewer friends. In an intriguing study, Sheldon Cohen at Carnegie Mellon University questioned volunteers in detail about the extent of their social ties before exposing them to nasal drops containing a rhinovirus, the common cold. The volunteers were then kept in quarantine for five days to allow the medical team to swab and analyse their mucus. The research team found that individuals with a greater diversity of social ties were less likely to get infected by the cold than people with fewer social ties.[95]

The number of friends people professed to having didn't make a difference to how likely they were to pick up the virus. Instead, the protective factor seemed to be the number of *different* social circles that people belonged to. The protective effect of social ties held even when the researchers took into account other factors including patterns of smoking, alcohol consumption, physical exercise, sleep quality and diet, and personality type. So when it comes to the shielding health benefits of social ties, both the quantity and quality of ties matters less than the sheer diversity of them, i.e. having more weak ties.

So by all means connect with friends and people you feel comfortable with. But remember that it's actually our weak ties that may help us to break fresh ground, achieve our goals, *and* protect our health. Whether you're looking for an unadvertised job opening, a new customer for your business, even an introduction to a hot date or just to live a healthier life, you're more likely to find it through casual acquaintances than close friends.

We shouldn't really be surprised that building social bonds to new people and associating with the right kinds of people helps us to achieve our goals. After all, human nature is fundamentally social. We live in groups and evolved to live in groups. But when the pace of modern life conspires against our relationships, remember that it's up to us to do the reaching out.

Onwards and upwards

Connecting is the skill of reaching out to new people and leveraging relationships for mutual gain. You don't have to meet hundreds of new people – even adding a few new contacts into your address book can make a difference and significantly boost your chances of achieving your goals.

- Savvy individuals appreciate that both the quality *and* quantity of relationships matter. The more people we meet and the more often we meet them, the more likely we are to engage with people who have overlapping values and interests. So get out there. Pick up the phone, and meet up in person. Renew old acquaintances and establish a few new ones.

- Remember that many people may be happy to help us to achieve our goals. But they can't unless we gently let them know we exist and tell them what we're about.

- Look to surround yourself with a group of people who are like the person you would like to become. Whether you want to lose weight, raise money for a cause, or yank yourself up into senior management, learn from people who are doing what you want to do.

- People are remarkably adept at seeing through falseness so think net*friending*, not networking. Seek genuine connections, look to be helpful, and make friends rather than trying to secure relationships only because they could be beneficial to you.

SIX

DARING

'The greatest mistake a man can ever make
is to be afraid of making one.'

Elbert Hubbard

SUPPOSE YOU WANDER INTO a friend's kitchen. You see a small dark blob of something that looks like food, but it doesn't look like anything you've seen before. Your friend is elsewhere so you sneak a taste of it. And it's delicious. Like nothing you've ever had before. To. Die. For.

Immediately, your mind whirls with ideas, possibilities. Your intuition tells you that there's a golden opportunity here. You don't know where it came from or how it's made, but you want to make it or import it or distribute it. You just want to get involved.

But you find out that you would need to buy expensive equipment to manufacture and sell it commercially. You'd need to raid your savings, beg friends and family for money, take a loan from the bank and *still* have to mortgage your home. Oh, and quit your job with no guarantee of success.

Still tempted?

Most people would pause, perhaps laugh nervously, and give up on the idea there and then. But not journalist Josephine Fairley. She succumbed to temptation and in that moment gave birth to Green & Black's, the premium quality chocolate business.

In the late 1970s and throughout the 1980s, Fairley was a thriving magazine editor and journalist. Aged only 23, she was the UK's youngest woman editor of a national magazine, in charge of *Look Now* and *Honey* before going on to become an accomplished freelance writer, for newspapers including *The Times*.

As the 1980s came to an end, she was enjoying her lifestyle as a writer, commanding respect from her peers and earning a good living. The last thing she expected was a total change in direction.

In 1991, she wandered into her husband's office and sampled a product she hadn't come across before. She ate a square of dark chocolate that was rich and sumptuous, totally unique, like nothing she'd ever tasted.

Her husband, Craig Sams, founder of the macrobiotic food company Whole Earth, was constantly trialling ingredients and testing new products. He'd been sent the chocolate bar as a sample, but didn't want anything to do with it. His company's ethos was championing products with no added sugar. Unfortunately the chocolate bar contained sugar – and without the sugar it was too bitter, completely inedible.

Fairley grasped the opportunity. She wanted to sell the product and build a business. Convinced that other chocolate-lovers would snap it up, she persuaded her husband to help her. He agreed to distribute and sell the product, but only if she would finance it and do all the marketing. Without any track record of selling a product, she spent £20,000 on 2,000 cases of the chocolate.

Why? Why did she take such a big bet on an untested product?

'I like a challenge,' she answers.

For years she had written about other people. She felt she had acted as a spectator to other people's fortune for too long. In that moment she decided it was time to do something herself.

'I bought a postcard in Carnaby Street when I was 15 or 16, of a man on a diving board that said, "If you don't do it, you'll never know what would have happened if you had done it." And actually that's always, always driven me.'

'In general I don't think it's a bad motto to live by. Fortune favours the brave or the bold,' Fairley adds.

She chose to name her company Green & Black's – 'green' because of the organic product and her environmental concerns and 'black' because the chocolate was the darkest, highest-quality chocolate on the market. The rest of the story is almost history.

Green & Black's grew at an astonishing pace, doubling in size year after year. Their Maya Gold product became the first Fairtrade-certified product in the UK. The company expanded quickly into organic cooking products, biscuits, and even ice creams. And in 2005, confectionery giant Cadbury bought the business for a sum estimated to be in the region of £20 million.

Fairley has since moved on to other projects – including buying Judges, an organic bakery, and founding natural health clinic The Wellington Centre, both in Hastings, East Sussex. However, she's still rightly pleased with the continuing success of the brand she created. In the latest CoolBrands survey, Green & Black's won the food category award, putting it in the enviable company of brands like Aston Martin, Dom Pérignon, and Jimmy Choo. 'Green & Black's is bigger than Marmite and cooler than Prada,' she informs me proudly.

Fairley is clearly intelligent and articulate. So what makes her different from all the other equally clever and eloquent people in the world?

Of course, she had a timely opportunity. But so many people talk about wanting to set up a business who never do it. Fairley actually gave it a go. When faced with the opportunity, she grabbed it with both hands.

Taking chances and embracing failure

No one sets out in life wanting to fail. But the top-performing people I interviewed spoke of the need to take chances, to take considered risks and be willing to accept failure as a part of learning.

When we're faced with new opportunities or uncertain options, many of us worry about what could go awry. But those dangers are more often in our heads than reality. Whether in our careers and business decisions, our personal pursuits or even our romantic lives, failure seldom leads to risk of life or limb. Failure is rarely final and almost never fatal – even though it may feel like it sometimes.

Of course there may be risks. But almost nothing in life is ever certain. While we might wish for the stars to align and conditions to be perfect, we could end up waiting for ever. Windows of opportunity don't stay open indefinitely. Other people may steal our great business idea, pounce on that exciting job offer, or ask out that dream date.

Often, the biggest risk is that we might look foolish or stupid should things go wrong. We don't want to suffer the scorn and 'told you so' derision of people we know. But embarrassment and even outright humiliation are just feelings; they can't kill us.

I define Daring as a willingness to take action in the face of uncertainty. It's about having courage and conviction, about pursuing opportunities in spite of how apprehensive or even downright scared we might feel. Daring is about embracing opportunities, forging ahead and not worrying about looking ridiculous should things go wrong.

Anyone can stay firmly within their comfort zone, eking out tiny improvements, perhaps a couple of per cent, in what they do every year. Even monkeys can learn a minor trick or two every year. But unless we risk wiping out from time to time, we aren't pushing ourselves. It takes a bit of audacity to lift ourselves from the throng.

One of the high achievers I've interviewed is Matt Roberts, one of the world's most famous personal trainers. He has shaped celebrity bodies including model Naomi Campbell, pop star Madonna, and fashion designer Tom Ford as well as kings, queens, and heads of state from all over the world. He's also used his personal profile to forge a multimillion-pound empire producing books, DVDs, clothing ranges, and branded gyms worldwide.

Even as a teenager, he began to take calculated bets. While many of his contemporaries left school to go to university, he decided not to pursue the safe route of an education at a British university. He instead studied courses through private companies and institutions both in the US and UK to become a sport scientist and physiologist.

He was only 22 when he invested all his money in opening his first gym, leasing a tiny space in Mayfair in the heart of London. This first venture was a smash and he found himself upgrading to larger facilities as well as opening gyms at the exclusive Le Touessrok and Le Saint Géran hotels in Mauritius. More than a decade on, he now has four personal training clubs in London in prestigious locations such as Hampstead and Chelsea and has plans to open at least a handful more over the next five years, either within the UK or elsewhere in the world.

But Roberts's story isn't one of untrammelled success. He argues that trial and error are part and parcel of being successful.

'If you try ten things and one comes off, you're doing pretty well,' he tells me.

'The key thing is that you have to not be afraid to try. I've invested money into things over the years which I thought were brilliant ideas that haven't come off.'

For example, he created a Matt Roberts-branded vitamin range for sale on the high street. He invested considerable time and money in selecting a manufacturing partner, designing the packaging, and marketing the product. However, the product never got off the ground. Over the years, he's also trialled products into his gyms including medical blood tests and yoga classes. He even toyed with introducing pods into his venues so stressed executives could power-nap during the day. That they didn't work out doesn't trouble him at all.

'Failure's okay. Failure is not a problem,' he says.

'You lose some money, you invested time and money into it, but it doesn't come off. That's the way it goes. You have to try and fail, understand why you fail and you grow from that and you don't do it again and do something that hopefully will work.'

Iconic people like Roberts are happy to experiment, to try new opportunities and options and see what happens. Of course they do their homework, weighing up pros and cons and calculating their responses to worst-case scenarios before they test the waters. They don't take foolish, breakneck gambles. But neither are they afraid to see their efforts flop or fail because they know they will learn from them and be able to move on.

Having the right regrets

American author Mark Twain once wrote: 'Twenty years from now you will be more disappointed by the things you didn't do than the ones you did do. So throw off the bowlines. Sail away from safe harbour. Catch the trade winds in your sails. Explore. Dream. Discover.'

Of course it's easy for an author to urge us to take more chances from the safety of his desk. Is it really true that you will regret what you didn't do rather than what you did?

Allow me to tell you Malcolm Green's story, a man who is in the business of emotions. He can make you feel happy or sad, wistful or even worried – and all in under 30 seconds. For over a decade he has been a creative director at world-class advertising agencies promoting, overhauling, or even rescuing dozens of big brands including British Airways, Vauxhall, Burger King, and eBay.

Chances are you've seen one of his award-winning campaigns. He had the flash of inspiration that brought together shy ex-England footballer Gary Lineker and Walkers Crisps in a campaign that so far has lasted 15 years – one of the longest running in British history. He also discovered Howard Brown, the bald, black, and bespectacled branch employee who sang his way through a seven-year campaign for the Halifax bank.

Green's creative career was almost cut short by a lack of self-belief. Even as a young child, he knew that he yearned to work in advertising. But his teachers told his parents that he was neither clever enough nor sufficiently industrious to go to university, let alone to work in advertising, back then one of the most prized professions for graduates.

He decided to give advertising a go anyway, managing to get his first job working in the post room and as a messenger boy. But he quickly discovered that working in the post room wasn't going to get him into the business of crafting adverts, so he moved on again and again, working at different agencies and eventually landing a job as an account executive.

'In advertising you have a choice between being creative or being a "suit", an account handler. I wanted to write the adverts but I didn't have the confidence. The creative people in those days were artistic types who'd been to art school and university. I'd done neither. I felt like an intruder, a gatecrasher.'

So he settled for life as an account executive. He watched his creative colleagues working their advertising magic while he went through the motions of his job, feeling frustrated but too afraid to switch to the creative side. The trajectory of his career looked to be taking him on a journey that was both so near and yet so far from his childhood dreams.

'I hated the job I was doing,' he admits.

Change came unexpectedly in the hours of darkness one December when he was only 22 years old. The night before Christmas Eve, he and three friends were driving home after a night out. A drunk driver smashed headlong into their car.

'We saw headlights which seemed to be on our side of the road. I was thinking, "He's going to crash into us," and the next thing I knew my heel was crushed behind my neck,' he says.

Tragically, two of his friends were killed in the collision and Green nearly died too. He broke his back, legs, arms, and most of his major bones. He was in traction for three months, giving him more than enough time to feel guilty, wishing that either all four of them had lived or that none should have survived.

But the experience gave him a fresh attitude.

'When you've got ambulance and fire people cutting open the car and saying, "He's going," about you, you think, "I'm dying, I'm going to die here." Even though you're drifting in and out of consciousness, you think about life. I remember it very, very vividly and the thing I remember was regretting the things I hadn't done, hadn't said. And not having done the things that were important. I didn't regret any of the mistakes I'd made,' he recalls.

'I thought, "Why should I do a job that I didn't want to do, watching people doing the job I did want to do?"' he adds.

Green attacked his career with new-found gusto and, although it took him a year, got a job as a copywriter at Saatchi & Saatchi, at the time the highest-profile advertising agency in the country.

'That experience drove me. It changed me, no doubt about it. It's a lesson that adversity gives you opportunity. Doesn't mean you want to have that experience, but I think that out of the downs, you can use them as a springboard for the ups,' he says.

And his career did go up. He was the youngest ever joint executive creative director at McCann Erickson. He won industry awards, prizes, honours. He remortgaged his home and sold his car to buy into a small advertising agency. Renaming it Delaney Lund Knox Warren, he and his business partners grew it from under a dozen employees to an organisation of over 300 people earning upwards of £110 million a year. And when they sold the company to a larger marketing conglomerate, he is rumoured to have netted a seven-figure cash payout. Not bad for someone who was told that he wasn't clever enough to make it in advertising.

People like Green have dramatic experiences that change the lens through which they look at their lives. They receive a new outlook and resolve to pursue what they want and live without regrets. What about the rest of us though?

Cornell University researcher Thomas Gilovich has studied the psychology of regret for many years. Asking people about the biggest regrets they had in life, he observed that 75 per cent of people regret *not* doing something as opposed to only 25 per cent of people who regret doing something.[96] Sure, in the short term people beat themselves up or feel angry about the actions they've taken that didn't turn out well. But in the long term, most people are more troubled by the regrets they have over what they didn't do and wished they had.[97]

BECOME YOUR BEST: Finding the courage to act

Many people take too few risks in life, seeking the safety of what they know. A few people, on the other hand, gamble too often, throwing themselves into situations that they aren't ready for and occasionally putting themselves in real jeopardy. Daring is about finding the middle ground between the two, balancing the twin needs of thinking and action.

Consider the big decisions and opportunities you're currently faced with. Or perhaps you turned down tempting offers or opportunities in the past. Looking ahead to the future, what would you like to do differently? How will you live your life so you won't feel that you're missing out?

For the most part, it's not difficult to distinguish between soul-enriching risks and frankly dangerous ones. Ran Kivetz, a professor of business at Columbia University, suggests the following mind hack: if you have a decision to make, imagine yourself 10 years from now, looking back on the decision. When you're looking back at your life from a broader perspective, what choice will you feel *glad* to have made?[98]

Surveys tell us that we're three times as likely to experience sorrow over omission (what we didn't do but we wish we had) than commission (what we did but wish we hadn't). We grieve over the opportunities we didn't pursue rather than the mistakes we made. Perhaps those regrets include people we wished we'd asked out, jobs or trips abroad we should have taken, qualifications we could have studied for, and all manner of routes and roads we glimpsed but didn't follow.

Too many people settle for what they have. Will you end up settling too?

Getting started

No one wants to sit on the sidelines of their own life, watching other people do exciting things, get the glory, and succeed. We want to be in the game and pursue exhilarating opportunities too.

So let's get started. I can't wave a magic wand to transform your life and give you everything you could ever dream of. But I can tell you that a vast body of research shows that people who set goals are much more likely to take action and make positive changes than people who only have vague intentions.

So let me take you through the psychology of goal setting, which shows us that the most motivating and effective goals tend to have four distinct characteristics. And here they are.

Positive

I studied for my doctorate in psychology at the Institute of Psychiatry, part of King's College at the University of London. The head of our psychology department was the late Professor Jeffrey Gray, one of the most distinguished experimental psychologists of the twentieth century. In a career spanning several decades, he discovered that the brain has two separate motivational systems. The Behavioural Activation System triggers behaviour in response to the presence of reward, while the Behavioural Inhibition System restrains our behaviour when we sense the likelihood of punishment.[99] In other words, we are hard-wired to respond to signals of both reward and punishment.

Which of the two systems is more effective?

If you've ever trained a household pet such as a dog or read about how animal behaviourists train dolphins, you'll know that reward is always better. Animals respond much more positively and learn more quickly when rewarded for the right behaviours rather than punished for the wrong ones. And the same goes for humans.

For example, a University of Rochester study found that people who set themselves avoidance goals (i.e. trying to get away from negative consequences) actually experienced a dip in their self-esteem and feelings of life satisfaction as compared with people who pursued approach goals (i.e. trying to move towards positive consequences).[100] A similar investigation looking at students' attempts to make new friends found that positively phrased goals such as 'wanting to make friends' were associated with better outcomes than negative goals such as 'wanting to avoid feeling lonely'.[101]

Ambitious and specific

Researchers Edwin Locke and Gary Latham have spent 35 years researching goal setting and how we can best motivate ourselves. In a summary of their work, they found that 'specific, difficult goals consistently led to higher performance than urging people to do their best'.[102]

At the same time, however, they found that goals that were *too* arduous could hurt performance. When people don't feel they have a hope in hell of achieving a goal, they give up. So while a goal needs to be somewhat stretching, ambitious, and even audacious, it can't be so daunting that it feels impossible.

Of course what feels challenging but not unattainable depends on the individual. For one person, getting up the courage to be able to give a speech at a wedding in six months' time could be plenty challenging enough. For someone else, the thought of running a business that spans, say, most of Asia may still not be thrilling enough.

We don't like to make liars of ourselves, either too. Setting specific goals can be helpful, too. So if, for example, you want to lose weight, specify that you will lose 15 pounds or drop two dress sizes. Or, if you want to raise money for a charity, state clearly that you will raise £5,000. Once that's done, you can't wriggle out of it. Tell colleagues that you're going to land a six-figure deal with a new client and you'll want to prove yourself right. Making ambitious, specific commitments is a great way to kick us into action.

Timed

I have a friend who frustrates me. Despite being an inordinately talented designer and wanting to start her own business, she can't seem to get around to it. When I ask her about when she'll do it, she always says something like: 'Oh, soon.'

When is 'soon' though? Next month, next year, next decade?

When it comes to doing chores, starting diets, looking for new jobs, and generally improving ourselves, we're all guilty of procrastinating occasionally. We also know from personal experience that externally imposed deadlines can provide us with some incentive or at least pressure to get things done. However, a research team from the Massachusetts Institute of Technology and INSEAD business school found that *self-imposed* deadlines boost our chances of getting tasks done too.[103] Deadlines don't have to be inflicted on us by people who will punish us for not doing them. Simply making a personal pledge to do a task by a certain date can be a good idea too.

BECOME YOUR BEST: Putting your future goals into the PAST

Use the PAST mnemonic to remember the four characteristics of effective goals:

- **Positive.** Set positive goals that help you to move closer to what you want as opposed to negative goals that try to move you away from what you don't want. A good goal should include language such as 'I want' or 'I will' as opposed to 'I don't' or 'I won't'.

- **Ambitious.** Too easy a goal and you won't get fired up about it. Too onerous a goal and you will simply give up. Try to set yourself a goal that stretches you, but won't snap you.

- **Specific.** Vague, woolly goals are too easy for us to squirm out of. Always seek to make as concrete and unambiguous a goal as possible.

- **Timed.** Create a realistic deadline for yourself – then stick to it.

Turning goals into actions

Great, we have a goal. What next?

When I'm working with clients, I don't recommend that they simply fling themselves into wholly new and potentially scary situations. No, I always advocate a little planning. By gradually building their skill one step at a time, they can give themselves the best chance of success.[104]

However, I sometimes discover that the biggest barrier to people's success isn't lack of skill or experience. It's not about getting the right training or qualifications. It's often psychological, about not having enough confidence to take those steps.

Thankfully we can build our confidence (and expertise) one step at a time. When we take even a small step towards our goals, we build what psychologists call our self-efficacy, our sense of personal power and the belief that our efforts can spark change in the real world. And when our self-efficacy increases, we feel more motivated and comfortable taking further steps. The more our self-efficacy builds, the more we can achieve.[105]

Imagine throwing a pebble off the top of a mountain. You might dislodge a handful of large stones. Those stones may in turn knock free a couple of bigger rocks. And the rocks may smash into boulders with enough force to cause an avalanche. When we take action – even when those actions are initially quite small – we can often trigger much, much more.

BECOME YOUR BEST: Taking a stepwise approach

If there's something big that you want to achieve in life, you probably won't get there in one go. Whether it's something to do with your career or personal life such as getting fitter, spend a few minutes planning ahead to rally your resources and help yourself to succeed.

Begin by drawing a staircase on a sheet of paper. It doesn't matter how many steps you give yours for now, although I'd include at least a half-dozen to begin with.

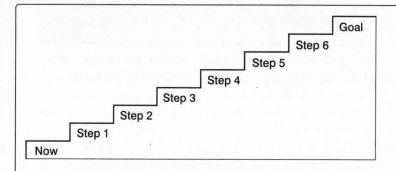

Write a few words about your current situation at the bottom of the staircase and a short description about where you'd like to get to at the top. Then start working backwards from your goal to figure out the individual steps you'd need to take. For example, you may need to put some money aside in preparation for your new pursuit or venture; you may need to refresh your skills, accrue certain experience, gain new qualifications. Perhaps you need to research your idea or meet particular people such as investors or clients. Or if you're trying to beat your fear of giving speeches in public, your first step may be practising a speech at home before giving speeches to a friend or two, then a handful of colleagues, the whole team, the entire department, and so on.

Think about the order of the steps. Which ones do you need to do first to help you out with the later ones? For each step, also be sure to consider:

● What are the specific actions you need to do?

● Who can/should help you?

You may have to redraw your staircase a couple of times, adding further steps, but that's okay. The exercise isn't about getting to the answer in one attempt. Every time you add a new step, you may think of more things you may need to do. The point is to cover all of your options and make your journey as smooth as possible.

But drawing your staircase is the easy bit. Now you have to take a deep breath and start doing it.

Doing as we believe

When it comes to taking action and achieving our goals, a huge part of success is psychological, to do with our mindset and the beliefs we hold about ourselves. If we have positive beliefs about our capacity to improve and grow, we *will* improve and grow. But if we doubt our own powers, we will hamper ourselves and struggle.

So let me ask you: to what extent do you believe in yourself – in your ability to develop your skills, grow your confidence, and advance in the world?

Stanford University researcher Carol Dweck has spent more than two decades looking at how people view their own abilities. She distinguishes broadly between two camps of people. One group has what she calls an 'entity' or static theory of ability, presuming that intellectual abilities are fixed. Other people believe in a 'malleable' or dynamic theory of ability and suppose that our mental skills are fluid, that they can be improved with discipline and practice.[106]

How does that help us? To show you why the distinction matters, let me tell you about a couple of experiments that tried to modify people's beliefs.

In the first study, investigators from the University of California at Berkeley coaxed volunteers to participate in an exercise to test their effectiveness as negotiators. Given a hypothetical scenario and a partner to negotiate with, they were awarded a score depending on how well they did, with the maximum score being 13,200 points.

Immediately before going into the negotiation tests, participants were randomly assigned to one of two conditions. In an 'entity' condition, participants were made to read a passage as follows:

Negotiation Ability, Like Plaster, Is Pretty Stable Over Time.

While it used to be believed that negotiating ability was a bundle of potentialities, each of which could be developed, experts in the field now believe that people possess a finite set of rather fixed negotiating skills. In most of us, by the age of ten, our negotiation ability has set like plaster and will never soften again.

The other half of the participants in a 'malleable' condition were made to read the following passage:

Negotiation Ability Is Changeable and Can Be Developed.

While it used to be believed that negotiating was a fixed skill that people were either born with or not, experts in the field now believe that negotiating is a dynamic skill that can be cultivated and developed over a lifetime. No one's negotiation character is hard like a rock that cannot be changed.

Participants in both conditions then went into the negotiation exercise and were scored. You can probably guess where this is heading. Participants in the 'entity' condition, who read that negotiation ability was fixed and unchangeable, on average scored a mere 3,332 points. Participants in the 'malleable' condition, who read that negotiation skill was fluid and open to improvement, on average scored a much more impressive 6,300 points.[107]

What astounds me about the study is that even reading a short paragraph of just over 50 words had such a formidable impact on people's effectiveness. People who believed in their ability to change and improve negotiated strongly; people who believed there was nothing they could do to improve fell far short of their potential.

I'm sure you believe – at least to some degree – in your capacity to change, grow, and improve your skills. But do you believe in your ability to change your intelligence? Do you believe that intelligence is something that's pretty much fixed by adulthood? Or do you believe that even our intellectual abilities are open to improvement?

In another experiment, a team of French and American researchers urged volunteers to complete a timed test measuring a single aspect, just one element of intelligence. Immediately prior to the test, participants were again randomly assigned to one of two conditions.

The 'entity' group were given the following paragraph to read:

In many studies, scientists have shown that: 1) Everyone has a certain level of this type of ability, and there is not much that can be done to really change it; 2) This type of ability depends on gifts or qualities that one has from birth; 3) Even if one makes an effort, one cannot really change one's ability level; and 4) This type of ability is not really modifiable.

They were also shown a chart with made-up data supposedly illustrating that even practice on such intelligence tests didn't improve performance.

In the 'malleable' condition, participants read a very different passage:

In many studies, scientists have shown that: 1) Everyone has a certain level of this type of ability, but there are lots of ways to substantially change it; 2) This type of ability does not depend on gifts or qualities that one has from birth; 3) If one makes an effort, one can change one's ability level; and 4) This type of ability is quite modifiable.

The 'malleable' participants were also shown a chart allegedly demonstrating that practice on such tests boosted performance.

No prizes for guessing what happened. Participants in the 'malleable' group performed significantly better than those in the 'entity' group. In other words, even on an intelligence test, people can be helped to achieve their potential when they feel that there's a reason to try harder. Reading even a short paragraph saying that we can improve our intelligence helped participants to work harder and get higher test scores.

So what's the lesson? Our beliefs have an enormous impact on the results we can achieve. That could be in our personal lives – perhaps trying to improve our proficiency at a particular sport or getting better with a musical instrument. That could be in a work situation such as improving our networking and selling skills or pushing ourselves to get a big end-of-year bonus.

Believe that we can't change and we naturally put less effort in and give up more quickly. But when we believe that we *can* change, we work harder, pay more attention, and actually do achieve more. As you can imagine, Daring is associated much more with having a malleable mindset, the belief that we can grow and that our efforts can lead to real improvements in our lives.

If you want to develop the malleable mindset that will help you to grow and improve, be sure to avoid attaching labels to yourself. Both positive and negative labels – such as 'I guess I'm naturally gifted with languages' or 'I'm just no good with numbers' – imply that your level of ability is fixed and un-changeable. Instead, remind yourself that we can all improve when we practise and make an effort.

BECOME YOUR BEST: Believing in our capacity to grow

Reading this book is a good start. Whenever you want to boost your motivation and reinforce a malleable view of your skills, return to this section of the book. Remind yourself that research tells us that when we believe in the dynamic nature of our abilities, we tend to work harder and produce better results.

Researchers have found that people can adjust their own beliefs about their abilities by writing a brief essay supporting the notion that people can change.[108] So if you want to supercharge your sense of confidence, your belief in your ability to change, try this exercise:

- Spend five minutes writing a short essay telling the reader how anybody can change, grow, and improve. Feel free to highlight examples you know from personal experience or to write about people you've read or heard about.

- Spend an additional few minutes writing out examples of how *you yourself* have changed. Recall instances in which practice helped you to get better. For example, what's a skill or subject area in which you once had low ability, but now perform better? Think too about attitudes you've changed, or experiences or qualifications you've gained. Even think back to the lessons you learned from mistakes you made.

Whether you're preparing for a challenge in your personal or work life, take 10 minutes to remind yourself of both how we can all change and how you have grown in the past. Perhaps you're studying for an exam or learning a new skill, preparing to take on a big project at work or poised to take on a daunting task. Whatever the case, help yourself to succeed.

Fostering Daring in others

Research on the fixed 'entity' mindset versus the dynamic 'malleable' way of thinking has important implications not just for how we can help ourselves to achieve our potential. We can help those close to us to be their best too.

In particular, we may be able to influence children and adolescents and help them to do better at school. A team of researchers from Columbia and Stanford universities found that teaching children about the malleability of their brains helped them not only to feel more motivated but also to get better grades at school as compared with children who had no such instruction.[109]

If you want your kids to work hard and do better, aim to:

- Teach them that our brain circuitry is malleable, that it forms fresh connections and grows in response to stimulation, and that nearly anything can be improved with diligence.

- Encourage them by reminding them that 'effort and hard work can help you to do better'.

- Reward your children when they do well by saying, 'You worked hard' (which reinforces the dynamic, changeable nature of their abilities) rather than 'You're so clever' (which implies that their abilities are an unchangeable gift that they were perhaps born with).

- At all costs abstain from using labels such as 'stupid' or 'rubbish', 'intelligent' or 'gifted'. Both negative and positive categorisations tend to promote a fixed view of the world, reducing the incentives for trying to break free of them.

But it's not only kids who may benefit. Savvy managers should similarly compliment members of their teams for their efforts and discipline; they should bring to wider attention instances in which people get better at a skill through practice and hard work. Husbands and wives, too, could help and encourage their partners to lose weight, stop smoking, and learn new proficiencies by congratulating them on their hard work whenever they see positive results. Whenever we know that people are trying to improve themselves, we should emphasise again and again how their efforts and exertions are directly causing the improvements they're seeing.

Learning to fail forwards

Pursuing more opportunities necessarily means that we will stumble and make more mistakes. And we should be ready for them. Exceptional people see blunders and failures as feedback, constructive criticism, and insight into what doesn't work or what they should do differently. Rather than seeing them as a sign that we should give up, setbacks can tell us that we may need to work harder, learn more, consider other options or adapt our tactics, or ask for help.

Repeated failures may tell us that we should perhaps pursue different paths – but then at least we know for certain what doesn't suit us rather than wondering what might have been. Time and again, the high achievers I interviewed told me how they learned not by shirking situations but by forging ahead and seeing what happened.

BECOME YOUR BEST: Having a Setback Manifesto

When things go awry, it's natural to feel upset or off-balance – and Centredness (see Chapter Four) is what helps high achievers to restore their emotional equilibrium. But success doesn't come from simply recovering and moving on as quickly as possible.

Too many people ignore their mistakes or look to place the blame elsewhere. Doing so means they risk making the same mistakes over and over again – clearly, not the cleverest way of going through life.

Virtuoso individuals make it a habit to review their mistakes and failures to learn what they could do better in the future. And, because we may not remember to do so, I suggest to the people I coach that they should have a Setback Manifesto, a short set of steps to work through when they experience a big setback.

When something important goes wrong, work through three simple questions:

- **What is a *constructive* way of looking at my reasons for failure?** We can choose to interpret any setback in different ways. If you believe 'I'm not clever enough,' or 'I'm a lost cause,' then it would clearly be foolish to continue onwards. But if you believe 'I need more support,' or 'I need more preparation next time,' then that points to the fact that you may need to ask for help or practise more first. Rather than internalising failure and blaming yourself, get used to looking for outward causes of failure. Ask yourself: 'What other factors – ones that aren't about me – might have contributed to this situation?'

- **What steps or actions should I take to reduce the likelihood of things going wrong in the future?** This next question is about preventing the situation from reoccurring. To avoid typos, for example, a manager might introduce a policy about always having two people proofread crucial documents before they go out to clients. Somebody who blurts out inappropriate comments in social settings might make an effort to listen more and speak less. Someone who gave a terrible presentation could invest in more preparation and rehearsal. The key is to decide on options that work for us as individuals.

- **What would be a more productive way of behaving should the same situation crop up again?** Even with the best intentions and lots of preparation and planning, we may still sometimes find ourselves repeating the same gaffe or falling into a similar trap. Imagining ourselves as objective bystanders to our own situations, what advice would we give ourselves? In what ways would we act or speak or behave differently?

Exceptional people don't scold themselves over and over again for mistakes or failures. Once you've spent the few minutes working through these three questions, move on. Focus on the actions you can take. Better to improve your skills or practise more than simply replay the situation endlessly in your head.

Onwards and upwards

Daring is a willingness to take action even though the results can't be guaranteed. It's about taking chances and accepting there'll be an element of risk to everything we do. But we do it because we'll learn from whatever happens rather than holding ourselves back because of worry about looking foolish. Bear in mind that even small changes to how you approach opportunities could make a big difference to what you can achieve:

- Remember that almost nothing in life can ever be certain. High achievers believe in trial and error and take action even when matters are uncertain or they feel a little scared. Fix in your mind the fact that more people regret what they *didn't* do rather than what they did.

- Set PAST goals. Research indicates that effective goals are Positive, Ambitious, Specific, and Timed. Then list the individual actions you should take to achieve those goals and start doing them. Action creates momentum. And momentum leads to results.

- Remember that a huge part of success is psychological, about the mind games we play with ourselves. Our beliefs can either help or hinder us in achieving our goals. Remind yourself of ways you've changed, grown, and improved to maintain the right mindset to sustain future efforts.

- Look for constructive ways to review setbacks and failures. Thinking, 'I'm a no-hoper,' or 'My boss won't let me do it,' will make your confidence and motivation shrivel; believing 'I need more practice,' or 'I'll ask other people for support,' will inspire you to keep going.

SEVEN

CITIZENSHIP

'Integrity is doing the right thing, even if nobody is watching.'

Anonymous

SAY YOU NEED A PLUMBER to do some work in your home, perhaps to fix a boiler or install a new bathroom. Through friends, you find your way to two plumbers who are available and you ask them both to quote for the job. Plumber A quotes £1,200 while plumber B quotes a mere £900. But you hear on the grapevine that plumber B may cut corners by using inferior materials and sometimes uses cheaper, toxic glue in his work. It's only a rumour through friends of friends rather than substantiated truth. Who would you pick – the more expensive A or corner-cutting B?

No contest, surely.

Both individuals and organisations are facing ever more scrutiny for their behaviour. One of the people keeping an eye on the reputations of large companies is Karen Fraser. As creator of the Ethical Reputation Index, an extensive survey of consumers' attitudes towards 50 major organisations, she has become a leading authority on corporate reputation.

Writing in the *Harvard Business Review*, she pointed out that 44 per cent of the 1,300 consumers she polled had spoken about corporate ethics with friends, family, or colleagues in the previous month. Their concerns included issues such as the exploitation of workers in developing countries and corporate practices that were harmful to the environment. Perhaps more importantly, though, nearly one in four consumers were conflicted. They continued to buy products and services from companies whose ethical reputation they deemed poor or very poor. However, they were poised to switch their allegiance the moment a convenient alternative came along.[110]

Putting it another way: the moment a better, more ethical choice becomes available, organisations that don't have an ethical reputation could easily find themselves losing up to a massive 25 per cent of their customers. Ouch.

I met with Fraser and sought her insights into the minds of consumers.

'The first thing that really struck me was that consumers are far more aware and interested in ethical issues than I'd imagined before we conducted the study,' she tells me.

She points out that retailers such as Marks & Spencer and L'Oréal-owned The Body Shop as well as breakfast cereal company Kellogg's and the BBC are ranked amongst the top 10 ethical brands. Organisations carrying a reputational risk for the near future include oil company Shell, airline Ryanair, and fast-food purveyor McDonald's, which all ranked in the bottom five of the 50 companies rated by consumers.

She recognises that people's attitudes towards companies don't automatically affect their purchasing behaviour. However, she suspects that the situation will change in the imminent future.

'From what I've observed, consumers' expectations have increased and will continue to do so and that will affect the way that we all do business. There will be a greater requirement for transparency and a greater requirement for ethical practices.'

Plus she has a stark warning for companies that behave in nefarious ways: 'Mud sticks. If an organisation has been involved – or perceived to be involved – in dodgy dealing in the past, people don't forgive them very easily.'

For example, Fraser tells me about one international bank that was perceived to have supported the apartheid regime of racial segregation in South Africa in the 1980s. More than two decades on, she found that consumers still recalled the press coverage. Even younger consumers who had barely been born at the time of the events had somehow become familiar with it.

'I think that ethical and sustainability issues are becoming more important. Web-based communications have accelerated that over the last ten years because consumers can share opinions in seconds. So if your company is involved in something that consumers dislike or disapprove of, the message can circle the world in a matter of seconds.'

People have always shared gossip and news about each other. We're not stupid. We don't simply accept what people claim about themselves. We realise that people exaggerate, cover up the truth or even tell outright lies about themselves. So we trust the judgement of third parties. We take note of reports and rumours, both positive and scurrilous.

But in today's digitally connected world, reputations matter more than ever. No longer must we rely on word-of-mouth missives from people we actually know. We don't have to wait for the mainstream media to uncover what we'd like to know. We can now turn to blogs, YouTube, and social networking sites such as Facebook, LinkedIn, and Twitter. Tap a company name or product brand into any search engine and a dozen results pop up.

Information about organisations can be transmitted around the world almost instantaneously. More and more, their every move is documented in web space. Whether they like it or not, reports, photos, and even videos are uploaded, categorised, and tagged. And such wisdom and warnings linger as nearly permanent reminders of the actions we all take.

Linking behaviour and reputation

Of course organisations have to be careful with their reputations. But increasingly we need to be protective of our individual reputations too. Reputation on an individual level matters because people like people like themselves. People have always talked about each other, sharing both positive recommendations and the most damning of evaluations. People gravitate towards individuals who have similar values to themselves; they shun people who violate ethical and moral codes.

Whether we're looking for a plumber to fix a leaky kitchen sink, a care home to look after an elderly relative, or an advertising agency to launch a new product, we trust recommendations about who's good and who's not. Even when we're wondering whether to accept a job for a new boss, we can't help but be swayed by what colleagues may have heard about him or her.

Scientists have found that certain areas of the brain are hard-wired to process moral and ethical behaviour. When people see or hear about behaviour that breaches their sense of right and wrong, they are steered by their emotions to avoid the transgressors. Writing in the prestigious journal *Science*, University of Virginia professor Jonathan Haidt notes: 'People in all societies gossip, and the ability to track reputations . . . is crucial in most recent accounts of the evolution of human morality. The first rule of life in a dense web of gossip is: Be careful what you do.'[111]

Because the best way to protect one's reputation is to behave in the right way. The capability of Citizenship is about living by a code of ethics, a set of values. By being good citizens, we draw like-minded people to us, the kind of people we crave as colleagues, customers, employees, and even friends. When we're seen in the right light, it materially affects the relationships we can build and ultimately the results we can achieve.

Surely we all aspire to live and work with people we trust and respect? We want to collaborate and be surrounded by people who want to do the right thing, who are principled and ethical and consider the long-term interests of as many people as possible. Nobody wants to struggle through life competing with everybody else because they see you as someone with dubious motives who pushes your own agenda no matter the costs to anybody else. Because that's what is at stake here.

As consumers, we don't buy from abusive, polluting corporations. And when we deal with people one-on-one, we don't buy from (or have much to do with) abrasive, poisonous individuals.

All of the exceptional people I interviewed for this book have astounding reputations. To ensure that nobody could feign to be something that they aren't, I asked clients and friends for recommendations of people whom they rated and perceived to be high achievers. In their respective fields and industries, every single one of the interviewees for this book garners wide respect and admiration.

But you know what? Not one of these individuals talked about how they cover up their misdoings or misdemeanours. Not one of them talked about the importance of massaging the messages they send out.

Because the best way to be perceived as good is to *be* good. The easiest way to be talked about in a positive way is by *behaving* in a positive way. They all strive to do well by others and focus on conducting themselves in responsible, ethical ways.

Citizenship is not about putting a gloss of apparent goodness on something that's broken or slapping a positive public relations slant on a story that's fundamentally untrue. It's about being that ethical, responsible, trustworthy person – not just pretending.

Question is: how? We're all faced with complex decisions and have precious little time to consider the consequences of our actions. So how can we guard our reputations and make the best of ourselves?

Thankfully, being a good citizen isn't demanding in the same way as learning a foreign language or doing calculus in your head. We all have the ability to be a good citizen, to think of the broader implications of our actions.

OVER TO YOU

Reputation is what people say about us when we're not there. And how they see us dictates how they will treat us, whether they want to work with us or even be in the same room with us. Exceptional people clearly have outstanding reputations. But how do people see you? If you can pick only five words to describe yourself, what would those words be? Of course, we can choose whatever words we like to say about ourselves, so it's not much of a test really.

Now, if you're brave and really want to learn about yourself, repeat the exercise with a handful of friends and colleagues. What five words would they use to describe you? And what does that say about you and your reputation?

I work with a particular multinational bank with tens of thousands of employees in countries from Europe and the Americas to the Middle East, Africa, and Asia. Every five or six years, the bank's senior leaders review its competency framework – the behaviours they believe all of their employees need to display for the bank to continue to grow and prosper.

A couple of years ago, the bosses introduced a new competency which they called 'The Right Thing'. They defined it with the following bullet points:

- Upholding the positive reputation of our organisation even at the expense of financial gain.

- Displaying personal integrity, doing what we say, and demanding the same from others.

- Behaving in an ethical, responsible fashion even when we believe others are not watching.

- Considering our wider impacts on the communities and environment in which we operate.

- Making decisions that we are proud of and which stand the test of time.

- Rewarding ethical behaviour over behaviour that is merely financially lucrative.

This bank is concerned with making money. That's what banks do. Their annual profits are measured in billions rather than millions of dollars, pounds, euros and yen. And their key objective will always be to generate revenues and profits. But the senior people within the bank realised several years ago that having too narrow and short-term a view of making money could ultimately be counterproductive. More than ever, their fear is that an over-eager bank employee could get the whole business involved with a company that pollutes the environment or exploits child labour in a developing country. Or a company that uses toxic chemicals in children's toys or even inadvertently harms wildlife. Imagine the media frenzy, the public outcry!

Behaving in an upstanding, ethical way is nothing new. We admire and find ourselves being drawn to people who are trustworthy and honourable, who follow through on their promises and try to do good. Honesty and integrity go a long way not only in business but in all of our personal relationships and life decisions. No surprises so far.

But what the bank's bosses have grasped is that the concept of integrity is becoming broader. It's no longer about being ethical just in one's immediate relationships. It's also about thinking in much broader terms, about the community in its widest sense, and even the environment and how we use natural resources.

The bank's leaders were aware of the perils of being dragged into situations that could damage their reputation. So they introduced 'The Right Thing' competency in order to train their many employees to think about the wider and longer-term issues surrounding all of their decisions. Rather than focusing solely on short-term financial gain, they must all focus on the bigger picture, the reputational risks, and how the bank's brand could be sullied. Ultimately, it's about ensuring that not even one of their tens of thousands of employees would make a choice that could return to haunt the bank.

The head honchos in the bank insisted that the new 'The Right Thing' behaviours should be embedded into the day-to-day workings of the bank. Job hunters looking to join the bank are asked interview questions about their ethics and behaviour. Employees are evaluated for their ethical behaviour when it comes to annual appraisals and even promotions.

The bank isn't just paying lip service to social and ethical issues by putting glossy images on their corporate website. They have made a covenant to change the ways in which all of their many employees think about their activities. Of course they still want to make money – but only if it can be done in an ethical way. This sea change stems from a critical realisation from the people at the top that behaving ethically and responsibly is a vital part of protecting the bank's ability to continue to make money in the future. Since introducing the competency, the bank has prospered. Certainly, the bank has weathered much of the storm to hit the banking sector and has emerged as one of the stronger players.

This particular bank isn't the only organisation to put such ideals at the heart of what they do. Every year, I help a number of organisations to work out the competencies that they want to emphasise in their organisations. To avoid devising a set of behaviours that may meet current needs but become dated too quickly, I look at both what employees need to be doing now as well as in the future. So I ask senior people in organisations: 'What *will* people in this organisation need to do in the years to come?' Listening to their answers, I've definitely spotted a trend amongst leading organisations to have a view that is both broader and more far-sighted, which was another reason I decided to include Citizenship in this book.

OVER TO YOU

One way to become a better citizen is simply to ensure that the topic stays at the forefront of our minds. In a progressively transparent and technologically connected world, it makes sense to assume that just about everything we consider private could become public. We do send emails to the wrong folks and have more and more of our lives recorded and posted online.

Rather than trying to tack on a veneer of goodness, the best approach is just to be good. So whatever you're doing, ask yourself constantly: 'How would I feel if this got online?'

Living and leading sustainably

All of the exceptional people I interviewed for this book embrace the notion of Citizenship, of living by a code of ethics and values. However, I believe that the concept of Citizenship is becoming progressively broader. We must do well by not only the people we meet, but also the community in which we live and the planet we live on.

Large organisations have grasped the need to consider the broader and longer-term consequences of their actions and inactions thanks in part to the work of people like Karen Fraser with her Ethical Reputation Index. Smaller organisations will soon appreciate the importance of behaving ethically and as good citizens too. And a point will come in the foreseeable future when even individuals will have to embrace Citizenship or risk being shunned. We're not there yet, but the day will come.

We all have a choice. We can either act now and set ourselves up as examples of good Citizenship and draw like-minded people to us, or get left behind for being ethical laggards.

When I talk about the broader and longer-term issues of Citizenship, what that really means is the notion of sustainability. In its traditional sense, sustainability is the capacity to endure, to keep on going. But in recent years, the word has come to have a more specific meaning, implying the ability of both individuals and organisations to use the Earth's natural resources in a way that can continue for ever.

An influential United Nations report in 1987 called to attention the fact that, for the Earth to remain a sustainable system, it requires 'meeting the needs of the present without compromising the ability of future generations to meet their own needs'.[112] The issue is undeniably complex, encompassing not only how we use finite resources such as oil and gas, fresh water, and food stocks but also how we address social inequalities in the world that continue to leave hundreds of millions of people living below the poverty line.

I pressed my contacts for experts to guide me on the issue of sustainability. Remarkably, they all suggested the same company: SustainAbility, a highly regarded firm with offices in New York, London, and other major cities worldwide. Acting as both an independent think-tank and a consultancy, the firm's vision is to forge a just and sustainable world for both present and future generations.

'Our vision is dangerously innocuous, it's probably what you'd expect from an organisation like us,' SustainAbility CEO Mark Lee tells me.

He makes a distinction between traditional views on philanthropy and current views on sustainability, arguing that philanthropy is an 'end of pipe' approach to Citizenship. He explains by citing John D. Rockefeller, the founder of the Standard Oil Company and perhaps the richest person ever to have lived on the planet, having been the world's first billionaire way back in the 1800s. Rockefeller built a vast petrochemical business empire and *then* donated monumental sums to charity.

Lee, however, argues that the modern notion of sustainability requires a 'through the pipe' approach. Both organisations and individuals must think about the impacts they have on other people and the planet *while* they're building their empires rather treating them as an afterthought.

Makes sense. After all, we don't want people to think it okay to exploit child labour in building a thriving business and only then donate to children's charities. So neither should we deem it acceptable for people to harm the environment in accumulating their personal fortune and only then plant a forest or preserve a portion of coastline.

The notion of sustainability requires a focus not only on the existing generation but also on future generations. We want to give our grandchildren and their grandchildren at least as high a standard of living as we enjoy rather than robbing them of their future. That requires a longer-term view and a sense of stewardship to ensure we leave them with adequate resources.

Stewardship over what though?

Lee shows me data on the issues of sustainability. The 2009 Sustainability Survey by SustainAbility and independent polling firm GlobeScan quizzed 1,691 highly qualified experts from over 90 countries to identify what they saw as the most urgent sustainability concerns. The numbers following each issue are the proportions of the experts who saw the issue as either 'very urgent' or 'somewhat urgent':

- Clean water shortages – 93 per cent
- Climate change – 89 per cent
- Poverty – 84 per cent
- Loss of biodiversity – 82 per cent
- Food security – 76 per cent

Other issues on the list included global malnourishment and starvation (71 per cent of the experts saw it as either 'very urgent' or 'somewhat urgent'), diseases such as malaria and HIV/AIDS (66 per cent) and air pollution (also 66 per cent).

The issue of poverty and wealth inequality is of particular importance as commentators have pointed out that the greatest environmental damage is often caused by those at the extremes of the wealth continuum. While the relatively well-off people in the developed world consume too much, the poorest people on Earth resort to desperate, short-term measures to survive from day to day.[113]

I can't disagree with Lee's arguments. Of course organisations need to minimise their impact on the environment and try to do social good – or at least cause no harm – while they go about their business. SustainAbility works with global brands such as Coca-Cola, Nike, Nestlé, and Starbucks. These are mega-corporations that are heavily scrutinised by government agencies, newspaper journalists, and charity outfits. Their decisions affect millions of people in countries all over the world. But what about the rest of us who aren't the chief executives of multinational businesses? How can we each contribute to sustainability as individuals?

Lee tells me that he lives by a mantra of trying to model the behaviour he wants others to demonstrate.

'I hope I'm gradually changing my behaviours in ways that have a direct impact but also have an impact on the folks that I am around,' he says.

'Whatever you want people at any level to do, if you don't model the behaviour, then forget it. Individually, people can powerfully model behaviour that they believe is good without being prigs or being irritating and pushing it on others.'

As you'd expect for someone in charge of a company that consults on social and environmental issues, he travels as little by air as possible. He buys from ethical clothing producers, describing, to my surprise, Adidas, H&M, Nike and Gap as 'amongst the most ethical producers of clothing anywhere in the world today'. He tries to shop locally and personally hectors supermarket managers when he sees food being wasted. But his biggest private challenge has been his attempt to cut down on the amount of beef he eats.

'I've said that I have to give up beef. No matter how you go about beef production, it's terrible for the planet. While I haven't made the choice to be a vegetarian, I eat much less protein than I used to historically. And it creates an immediate point of conversation, right? Because people tend to ask, "Why? Is it for health reasons or because of sustainability issues?" It creates a bit of an opening, if you will,' he says.

The simple act of talking over issues with friends can often be the first stage in changing people's behaviour. Lee argues that we mustn't undervalue how much of the movement towards sustainability in all sorts of organisations has been led by consumers. And even junior employees within massive corporate behemoths can have significant sway when they repeat the same messages.

'The degree to which this has been groundswell from employees and to which senior leaders have been galvanised to finally do something about this because the next generations of employees have said, "Sustainability's an issue," just can't be underestimated. It doesn't take that many voices,' he adds.

So Lee's point is that living in a more ethical, sustainable fashion is something we can all get involved in. You don't have to be a chief executive to have sway over people. Big changes can begin at the grassroots level.

Your influence may simply be over several dozen friends and family or a handful of colleagues at work. Or perhaps you can influence hundreds of employees or even millions of customers. Doesn't matter. Citizenship isn't about how many people you influence; it's about being concerned about the messages you send and the ways in which you have influence over them. Irrespective of how many people you can influence, the principle is the same: in all areas of your life, set the right example.

'I try to find the balance in terms of being outspoken with friends and communicating what I believe in and care about but not irritating the crap out of them either. You can't just constantly carp on folks and expect them to change behaviour. They need reasons too,' Lee concludes.

In terms of a compelling rationale, everyone could do worse than to read *Sustainable Energy – Without the Hot Air*.[114] The book is written by David MacKay, a physics professor at the University of Cambridge and chief scientific adviser to the UK Department of Energy and Climate Change. He presents the facts about sustainability without the hype, emotions, and rhetoric thrown about by both campaigners and sceptics alike. Best of all, his aim in writing the book is to educate rather than cash in. So you can download the entire book legally and for free from the website: www.withouthotair.com. It's a bounty of information and cool-headed analysis – and it won't cost you a penny.

Doing good, getting rich

Working on sustainability issues perhaps still has a whiff of the tree-hugging, do-gooding activist about it, of someone who's on the fringes of society, eschewing modern-day comforts and conventional careers because they care about the environment. And private equity adviser Tom Hill-Norton certainly cares about the planet.

'I've always been interested in green issues. I was head of the green society at school, was a member of Surfers Against Sewage when I was very young, so it's something that I've always been interested in,' he tells me.

Having lived and worked in countries such as Brazil and Mexico, he has seen first-hand some of the environmental and social issues that affect developing nations. Telling me that he comes from 'a very privileged background', he feels a desire to use his education and the chances he has had to give back to the world.

But then he adds: 'From a human angle, I have a desire to try and solve those issues and if you can do that profitably, then all the better.'

Hill-Norton is about as far removed from the stereotype of an environmental campaigner as you can get. He has an MBA from the prestigious INSEAD business school in France, one of the top five business schools in the world, and has a CV that includes banking giant JP Morgan. From his offices in exclusive Mayfair in central London, he is one of the founding partners of Plane Tree Capital, an independent private equity firm established in 2007 to focus on investment opportunities in clean energy technologies.

When I ask him about sustainability, he is quite emphatic about the topic's importance. He argues that it's an issue that no one can afford to ignore for any longer.

'Your carbon footprint and the sustainability of the way you do business is just a factor that will become increasingly important in terms of how you recruit people, the suppliers you use, what your customers are looking for. From every angle, there's a collective consciousness that this is a key issue of our generation and those companies that ignore it will do so at their peril,' he continues.

He says that the opportunity to get involved in clean energy 'seemed like sort of the holy grail of something I had been looking for pretty much my whole career. It's a way to first of all make very successful investment and generate a lot of financial value for your investors, but secondly to have a very direct impact on development, environmental, and social issues.'

Plane Tree Capital is already involved in projects to do with harnessing methane gas released from landfill sites in developing countries to power turbines and generate electricity. Hill-Norton's team is also investigating small hydropower projects, using the natural power of river torrents to generate energy. Another opportunity involves generating electricity from the burning of bagasse, a by-product of the Latin American sugar cane industry after the sugar has been extracted. What all of these projects have in common is that they not only generate electricity and protect the environment, but are likewise set to make both Plane Tree Capital's investors and owners – including Hill-Norton – rich.

And why not? If Hill-Norton succeeds in his mission, he will be contributing to what's been called the triple bottom line of not only financial returns but also both social and environmental benefits. Make money, help people, save the Earth. It's a win-win-win situation for everyone involved. So the arguments for Citizenship aren't just about behaving in a way that protects one's personal reputation and the planet – it's also about either saving or making money from the opportunities that are to be had by wasting fewer natural resources.

'I'm someone who's looked at this sector for the last ten years and I'm still surprised that people still ask the question of whether there is conflict between sustainability and profits. If you take overall the figures and trends, the triple bottom line of environmental, social, and economic performance is what sustainability is all about: an economy that lasts, that creates jobs, that uses its resources more efficiently, and each feeds off into each other. It's not a trade-off. It's a self-reinforcing factor for a better-performing economy over the longer run,' Hill-Norton states emphatically.

His beliefs are consistent with a snowballing body of research.

For example, the Massachusetts Institute of Technology conducted a survey of more than 1,500 global business executives. The 2009 report concluded that most companies were not acting decisively on issues of sustainability. However, a minority of companies were 'acting aggressively on sustainability – and reaping substantial rewards. Once companies begin to act aggressively, they tend to unearth more opportunity, not less, than they expected to find, including tangible bottom-line impacts and new sources of competitive advantage.'[115]

Another study in the *Harvard Business Review* came to similar conclusions. University of Michigan business professor C. K. Prahalad and associates studied 30 large organisations and found that 'sustainability is a mother lode of organizational and technological innovations'. They concluded that: 'By treating sustainability as a goal today, early movers will develop competencies that rivals will be hard-pressed to match. That competitive advantage will stand them in good stead.'[116]

Which would you rather be, one of the exceptional first movers or one of the people that tries to play catch-up? The news is good for people willing to make the first move into living and working sustainably. Running a sustainable business doesn't just boost the reputation of that business; it's also a nifty way to make money.

Putting Citizenship into action

High achievers haven't always been good citizens in the past. But in our ever more transparent and sophisticated world, exceptional accomplishment and Citizenship seem to be converging.

Critics may argue that we could cope without Citizenship, that it's an optional extra, the icing on the cake rather than a core capability. But then we could contend that some people do succeed without Awe and the gift of creativity or Authenticity and the ability to find work they naturally find inspiring. We could choose to ignore any one of the eight capabilities in this book. But why hobble ourselves and hamper our chances?

Good Citizenship should pervade not only how we behave at work but also our private lives. It is a part of the actions and choices we make as consumers, parents to the next generation, members of our local communities, and inhabitants of the planet Earth. Citizenship is about focusing on our personal legacy – no matter how big or small – and on making decisions and taking actions that consider the broader and longer-term picture. So it's as applicable to a young student as it is to a senior executive in charge of a globe-spanning corporation.

Becoming a better citizen isn't rocket science either. We can all do it if we simply choose to think more deeply about our decisions. Research, for example, shows that supermarket shoppers tend to purchase items that are worse for the environment when they're under time pressure.[117] So simply taking a few more moments to weigh up the consequences of our intended actions or inactions may be all it takes to become a better citizen.

I'm sure you can think of people in the same profession as you who cut corners; they rely on charm and manipulation and putting a sheen on matters to get ahead rather than doing the job as it's supposed to be done. Yes, they may be able to get away with it – for now.

And yes, there are many things going on around us that we can't control. But we are all free to make choices – small decisions that influence those near us and perhaps those around them. Deciding, for example, to recycle your plastic bags will not in itself save the planet. But letting your friends see that you do it may inspire them and potentially some of their friends too.

BECOME YOUR BEST: Considering the bigger picture

At the heart of Citizenship is considering the broader and longer-term impacts of more of our decisions. There's no miracle pill or magic bullet for being a better citizen. But even a few minutes of additional thought may pay off immensely.

Imagine that you have a board of advisers who will oversee all of your decisions. Your panel is made up of three people:

- **Someone in your profession, a peer.** What would someone in your profession expect you to do? This first question is about considering the responsibilities and obligations to your field of work, your profession. For example, I am a chartered psychologist of the British Psychological Society. If I were to step out of line, I would expect my fellow psychologists to consider the evidence and decide my fate. But even if you don't belong to a professional body, simply consider what a dozen ethically minded peers doing the same job as you would do.

- **A close friend outside of your work who you respect.** We sometimes justify our actions because we argue that we 'have' to take certain actions because that's what's expected of us in our work. But what would a pal say who knows nothing about the technical nature of your work? Would they take a positive or dim view of your actions?

- **Your grown-up grandchild.** Transported through a rift in space and time, your descendant from 50 years in the future has been brought back to the present day to listen to what you have to say. How will you explain the decision you're about to make to him or her?

Refusing to buy cheap clothes made by a retailer that uses child labour – and letting people know of your decision to do so – may incite your friends to follow your example.

Even the media we consume can make a difference. Declining to engage in tittle-tattle sets a good example for our friends and children. Refusing to watch an exploitative TV programme and showing that you're above it may ultimately cause the ratings to fall and the TV channel to take notice.

Whether positive or negative, our actions can have formidable effects. Like ripples in a pond, the small splashes we make can radiate outwards and have widespread consequences. Exceptional people realise that good actions beget good results. How about you?

Onwards and upwards

Citizenship is the skill of not only protecting our reputation but acting to enhance it. People with the skill of Citizenship do more than just 'what they can get away with'; they do the right thing because they want to be seen as leaders rather than laggards. Here's a reminder of how you can get started:

- Humans have a highly evolved ability to judge the reputations of others. Consider that the best way to have a good reputation and draw like-minded people to you is by *being* good, by behaving ethically and responsibly with an eye for the bigger and longer-term impacts of what you do.

- Remember that Citizenship applies to all of us – from young people starting out in their careers with seemingly little influence to senior people with sway over thousands or millions of people. Regardless, the principle remains the same: make good decisions and set an example to those around you.

- Ethical, responsible behaviour will increasingly become a prerequisite for success rather than an optional extra. Consider that it's better to be thought of as a leader than an ethical idler.

- Being a good citizen simply involves investing a little more thought into the broader consequences of all that we do. Ask yourself: 'What would my children's children want me to do?'

EIGHT

VISIONING

'No one ever finds life worth living;
he must make it worth living.'

Anonymous

I COACH A MAN I'LL CALL JOHN SOUTER. That's not his real name for reasons that will become apparent. He worked for a government department as a junior manager until he was in his late thirties. When we first met, he had just quit and wanted guidance on setting up his own business. He had taken an idea for a software application to his bosses; they hadn't been interested because they couldn't see the immediate benefit.

That was over five years ago. Fast-forward to the present and he employs nearly 30 people in offices in Hong Kong, London, and Dubai. I won't go into what his software does, but he makes a lot of money from it. He rents an apartment in central London but bought a house in an up-and-coming district of south London that he currently has people renovating for him. He also bought a luxury car and hired a driver to chauffeur him around the UK when he's in the country. Shockingly, he had enough money but not the time to choose the car himself so asked his driver to choose a car, ending up with a Mercedes Benz.

Thing is, Souter isn't happy. For a start, he travels all of the time. Trying to fit coaching sessions into his diary is often a nightmare of scheduling and rescheduling. A not unusual month sees him travelling to Dubai, then London, then San Antonio in Texas, then back to Dubai, London, Singapore, and then Hong Kong before coming back to London. I have coached him in the back of his car on a journey to Heathrow airport because he had insufficient time to spare.

Then there are the events that unfolded at Christmas. He nearly died. On a week-long holiday abroad – his first all year – he collapsed after a drinking binge and was hopitalised. Back in the UK, his doctor told him that he had been lucky. He had extremely high blood pressure, brought on by a combination of stress and being very overweight. Another such event would kill him.

Thankfully, he now admits that his life isn't working. He's stressed and lonely. He has few friends, no hobbies or interests outside of his all-encompassing work. He'd like to be in a fulfilling relationship but spends so little time in the country and is often so tired and bad-tempered that he hasn't managed to maintain one.

From the outside, Souter seems to be a conspicuous success. He is his own boss, running a thriving business that generates seemingly limitless pots of cash. But his life is secretly broken.

In building his business, he clearly had vision, an idea of what he yearned to achieve in the future. He wanted to be rich, powerful, successful. But he realises now that his original vision was one-dimensional, flawed like a one-legged chair – precarious and ready to topple. He went from one extreme to the other, either working too hard in pursuit of his defective notion of future financial success or living too hedonistically in the moment. He had little by way of a life outside of the two.

Visioning is the skill of creating the right kind of vision, one that encompasses what we want from our whole lives and not just our careers. By doing so, we can ensure that we not only achieve our future goals and the rewards that go with it, but also enjoy the lives we live in the meantime.

Getting to grips with the vision thing

Corporate bosses, business school professors, and even community leaders talk about the importance of having a vision. So what is a vision – and why do we need one exactly?

American President John F. Kennedy famously had a vision in the early 1960s of putting a man on the moon, as a rallying call for advancements in engineering, science, and technology.

In 1969, Neil Armstrong became the first man to walk on the moon.

Consumer goods company Proctor & Gamble's vision is to: 'Be, and be recognized as, the best consumer products and services company in the world.'

The World Wildlife Fund (WWF) also has a short statement encapsulating its vision: 'We seek to save a planet, a world of life.' Writing on their website, president and CEO Carter Roberts explains further: 'Reconciling the needs of human beings and the needs of others that share the Earth, we seek to practice conservation that is humane in the broadest sense. We seek to instil in people everywhere a discriminating, yet unabashed, reverence for nature and to balance that reverence with a profound belief in human possibilities. From the smallest community to the largest multinational organization, we seek to inspire others who can advance the cause of conservation.'

Finnish telecommunications firm Nokia's vision is: 'A world where everyone can be connected.'

All of these visions are pictures of the future. They are designed to help employees or customers or communities to understand their organisations' goals and keep them motivated to push forwards and work towards achieving those goals.

A vision can be a loosely defined dream (like the WWF's 'We seek to save a planet, a world of life' and Nokia's 'A world where everyone can be connected') or a concrete target (like John F. Kennedy's goal of putting a man on the moon). But what they all have in common is that they combine images or ideas that excite people and stoke within them the desire to achieve something.

Having a clear vision of what they want to achieve helps people to prosper. There's proof. In one notable study, the University of Maryland's J. Robert Baum asked 183 entrepreneurs and CEOs whether they had a vision or not. Baum's research team then followed the leaders over a period of two years and gathered data on their companies' performance.

The results were clear: leaders who said that they had a vision helped their companies to grow significantly more than leaders who did not have a vision.[118] Even more impressively, when the study authors followed up the participants for a further four years – making six years in total – the relationship still held: entrepreneurs who had a vision for their businesses saw more growth than their counterparts without a vision.[119]

Imagination and intention

People have individual visions too. True, the average person on the street doesn't necessarily talk about 'having a vision'. But this book isn't about regular people. Exceptional individuals *do* speak of having a vision of the career, the life, and the legacy they'd like to carve out, and of the quests or goals that make them leap out of the bed in the mornings.

While many people wait for the future to unfold and simply hope for good things to materialise, high achievers *decide* what they want and work towards shaping their future.

Research tells us that even the mere act of imagining something can make it more likely to happen. One team of experimental psychologists invited volunteers to take a test that involved them solving word anagrams in a set amount of time. Immediately before taking the anagram test, half of the participants were urged to imagine that they had failed on the test and to explain why they might fail. The other half of the group were asked to imagine they had succeeded on the test and also to explain why they might succeed. Those who had imagined success actually did better on the test than those who had imagined failure.[120] Their mental expectations and explanations had a tangible effect on their performance.

Having a picture of our desired future can be a formidable force when it comes to our lives then. A vision is a handy way to gather our thoughts about the life we crave. What do we want to achieve? How do we want to be remembered? No matter the circumstances we find ourselves in, we can conceive of ways to make them better.

By considering some of the bigger questions, we provide ourselves with a way to stay motivated. When we have a bad day, it helps to have that bigger picture, a grander intent, to remind us why we're soldiering on and what our options might be. As Friedrich Nietzsche wrote: 'He who has a why to live can bear almost any how.'

Once we've identified what's important and what's not, we help ourselves to make better decisions and avoid veering off course too. Say you get offered a job with a bigger salary and a swanky office. If accepting the job will ultimately help you to achieve the vision of the person you want to be and the life you want to lead, then take it. But if you're tempted only because it's the expected thing to do – your friends would probably take it – rather than because it will help *you* to achieve your important goals, then turn it down.

When we need to make decisions in any area of our lives – our friendships and family relationships, our health, how we spend our money, and the legacies we wish to leave – a vision should act as a compass, pointing us in the right direction. Having spelt out a vision, we can quickly identify whether any given opportunity would make us thrive or suffer.

I talked about the importance of goals in Chapter Six on Daring. Research tells us that positive, ambitious, specific, and timed goals spur most people on to greater heights. However, a vision serves a different purpose. It allows us to make sure the goals we set are the right ones to have rather than barrelling after any particular goal just because it's expected of us. So while we can tick goals off, we should aim to have a vision that is slightly beyond our fingertips, a dream or aspiration that stretches us and encourages us on.

The clearer you are about what you want in life, the more likely you are to get it. People with a vision have a clarity and sense of purpose that helps them to stay on course.

So what might your vision look like?

OVER TO YOU

People are living longer. Only a couple of hundred years ago, 50 might have been considered incredibly old. But as science and medicine continue to make advances, it's not unreasonable to believe that we may live to be 100.

So spend 10 minutes picturing yourself at the age of 100. From that vantage point, consider how you would like your life to look. What would you like to have done, to have accomplished by then?

The right kind of vision

The idea of having a vision is hardly new. I meet many people who have a vision. But Visioning isn't just about having *a* vision. Instead, exceptional people – the happiest and most successful individuals amongst us – generate what I call balanced vision. Rather than just having a set of big goals that they aspire towards, they get the right mix of elements into their visions. They keep themselves inspired and motivated by creating an attractive yet achievable picture of the whole lives they want.

Take entrepreneur Julian Ranger, for example. Like many high achievers, he is a rich man. He set up his first business, military communications firm Stasys, in the late 1980s when he was 23 years old. When he sold the firm in 2005 to multibillion-dollar defence contractor Lockheed Martin, the business had 230 employees and a turnover of over £17 million. He can't divulge how much he earned from the sale, but he did afford to take his family on a year-long tour around the world to celebrate.

Perhaps part of his achievement can be attributed to the robustness of his vision. Many people have ideas of what they want to achieve, but Ranger is one of the few, exceptional individuals to write it down.

'I do believe it makes sense to have written goals. I think if you write them and put them above your desk or have them wherever else, then you will achieve them,' he tells me.

He has four major categories of goals: relationships, learning, experiences, and achievement. In addition, he has an overarching goal to do with 'order'.

'To me, order is having a clear idea of what my vision is, what I want to achieve, the projects and tasks I need to do to achieve those so things get done and don't get forgotten and to help stop me procrastinating. Without thinking about what you want, you will never achieve what you want to do,' he says.

His first category of goals is about the relationships in his life. He argues that people who are driven have a tendency towards selfishness. Having a category that is to do with his family first and friends second reminds him to make time for them.

'Otherwise it's very easy for everything else to run away with your time. When you ask most people about work–life balance, everybody always says, "Yes, I'd like more time with my family," but they just don't do it because they don't have a bloody great big sticker that says, "Action number one: family". So every Sunday when I review my goals, family is up there. We're one of those families that eats dinner together at a quarter to seven every single day.'

Learning is another key category. He argues that a major part of being a flourishing leader or entrepreneur is having a learning disposition, accepting that you always have new topics and ideas to learn.

'One of the questions I'm often asked as an entrepreneur is: "Where do you get your innovative ideas from?" The answer is that if you are always willing to read, learn, and study all over the shop and accept that you don't know everything, it just generates ideas. I need to read, browse the web, and have no particular purpose, just learning, just following where the data trail takes you, chasing down bunny holes, reading until your brain hurts and you think, "This doesn't make sense."'

On his recent reading list, for example, he tells me he has read a couple of business books, as well as books about parallel universes, physics, climate change, and the Antarctic.

Ranger defines his third category of 'experiences' as a range of activities that help him to feel alive.

'I love my sport, so rugby, cricket, diving. Holidays, travel, walking, going to the theatre, taking photographs,' he says.

He also intends to travel into space to fulfil a boyhood dream. But this isn't mere idle fantasy. He paid $180,000 to book a seat on Virgin Galactic, the space tourism service that many experts predict will be the first commercial business to offer flights into space. He's currently 152nd in the queue and has been told that he may get to experience the weightlessness of orbiting Earth as early as 2012.

His fourth and final category of goals is about achievement. Part of this is to do with his work. Having made his fortune in engineering, he continues to work as an investor and consultant to technology and engineering companies. For example, he is a major investor in and adviser to Astrobotic Technology, a company that aims to put robotic rovers on the moon to gather scientific data for commercial purposes.

However, his 'achievement' category isn't only about the businesses he runs. He also heads up a charity with the aim of encouraging more young people to study STEM (science, technology, engineering and mathematics) subjects while still at school. His goal over the next 10 to 20 years is to attract more school leavers into studying science and engineering degrees at university; his dream and perhaps legacy for future generations is to create more scientists and engineers who will make discoveries and build tools to benefit society and the world.

So how well does his holistic vision, his set of goals, work for him?

'We're all driven people. If you give me the chance, I will happily spend hours on one thing but to the detriment of everything else I want to achieve. Having the system allows me to achieve my goals. It stops me from being sucked away to one goal,' he explains.

Ranger exemplifies the capability of Visioning. He is a fiercely passionate man who knows his zealousness can run away with him. So he has concocted a well-rounded, complete vision of the whole life he craves – not just the career and work achievements he wishes to pursue. And, rather than having a vision that gets shoved away into a drawer, he reviews his life against it weekly, reminding himself of his priorities and making sensible trade-offs. So even though, for example, he may need to work long hours in bursts, he never does so in an unsustainable fashion, in a way that might wreck his overall life.

OVER TO YOU

Identify three people you admire who seem to have successful, fulfilled lives. What is it you admire about them? Spend a few minutes jotting down a few ideas on what can you learn from them or incorporate into your own life.

Defining success

What's in your vision of a successful life? What would you consider a life that has been prosperous and well lived?

I work with a lot of talented, ambitious managers and entrepreneurs. They all earn significantly more than the national average – most earn six figures and some reach into the high six figures – but I'm afraid to say that they aren't necessarily happier because of their earnings. Despite having the outward, material trappings of success, they often tell me that they don't *feel* successful. Relentless, unbridled ambition can sometimes have its costs.

Many driven people define themselves too strongly in terms of their career and financial success. Without even consciously realising it, they often judge themselves based on whether they earn enough or have the right job title. They are hungry to earn more, kicking themselves for not getting the big promotion, hoping that more financial attainment will make everything right.

I coach more than a handful of people who have a mental attitude that I call Destination Fixation. These individuals believe that success is solely a future event, a destination that they need to reach. They see success as something they currently don't have – but will have once they get a particular promotion, earn a certain amount or achieve some other concrete goal. They make all sorts of sacrifices – perhaps to their health, relationships, even their sanity – to achieve the impending goal. Underlying their behaviour is often a belief that all they have ever wanted will come to them at the moment they achieve their goal. It's a form of perfectionism, of wanting everything to be perfect before they can start living their lives properly. But of course perfect never arrives.

Individuals with Destination Fixation often don't see it in themselves without a lot of introspection or having it pointed out. Because once they've hit the goal, they simply get used to what they've got, revise the goal upwards and push themselves onwards yet again. They perpetually sacrifice in the present – feeling tired, grumpy or even miserable on a daily basis – in their quest for a future that will never fully deliver what they hope for. What's the point of all the work if the end result is yet more work?

Certainly, research shows that people who strive for a particular salary level in the belief that it will make them happy rarely do achieve contentment. Instead, they get used to that level of affluence – in psychological parlance, they habituate – and start to hanker after the next level of income. In a survey conducted by an American newspaper, people who earned less than $30,000 a year believed that $50,000 would fulfil their dreams. Those with incomes of over $100,000 felt they needed $250,000 to be satisfied.[121] Get what you thought would be enough and you may just end up wanting more.

The best evidence of a disconnect between money and contentment comes from a study by research psychologists led by Ed Diener. They surveyed multimillionaires (who each had an average net worth of $125 million – in other words, quite a lot of money) and found that they reported only marginally higher average happiness than people on average incomes. Most astonishingly, though, more than a third of the multimillionaires were actually *less* happy than the national average.[122] Seems that money really *can't* buy happiness. Being rich isn't the same as having a rich life.

Economists talk of the declining marginal utility of money, the notion that the more we possess, the less each additional unit is valued.[123] And indeed an economic analysis by Aaron Ahuvia, a professor of marketing at the University of Michigan-Dearborn, estimated that income explains only between 2 and 5 per cent of the differences in subjective well-being amongst people in developed countries.[124] For most of us, then, between 95 and 98 per cent of how we feel about ourselves has little to do with how much we earn. So surely a balanced vision has to reflect that? Otherwise, we could easily chase financial prosperity but never *feel* successful or fulfilled.

Few people believe they have lives that are out of kilter. Most determined people believe they're on the right track and that issues like Destination Fixation couldn't possibly apply to them.

But then we may not always be the best judges of ourselves. Researchers call this the 'above average effect' – we tend to ignore our own flaws and believe we're better off than most people.[125] If you want to check how balanced your life is, get a second opinion. Ask your closest friends and members of your family, or partner and children (if you have them): 'How balanced is my life? To be the best parent/partner/human being I aspire to becoming, what could I be doing differently?' And if you're not willing to ask them, might it be because you already suspect the answer?

Making conscious, deliberate trade-offs

I'm not saying that we must never pursue higher earnings, career attainment, and more responsibility. However, we may perhaps need a clearer appreciation of what we want, why we want it, and what we hope it will bring. We can all benefit from disentangling what is genuinely important to us from the values of those around us.

A lot of ambitious people spend less time defining success than they spend racing blindly towards it. Without clear measures, we can risk running, rushing, and driving hard with no destination. Like getting into a car and hurtling along the street as fast as we can with no appreciation of where we're going.

The exceptional people I've interviewed or worked with appreciate that a successful life – *feeling* successful and fulfilled – isn't about hitting particular targets or milestones in the future.

They realise that success also comes from thinking about the life they lead in the present too.[126] Because life is a zero-sum game. We only have 24 hours in a day. Spend an extra hour at work every day and that's one less to spend catching up on sleep, making love to your partner, or exercising and eating more healthily.

We can appreciate that having a membership to an exclusive gym isn't the same as being fit and healthy if you don't put in the effort. Similarly, having a partner isn't the same as *being* a good partner. Having children is not the same as *being* a good parent.

Let's talk about our children for a moment. Some of my most ambitious clients believe that earning more money will provide security and happiness for their families and kids. But that's not always the case. An investigative team at Columbia University found that the children of affluent parents were at *higher* risk of clinical anxiety and depression than the children of less well-off parents. The researchers suggest that one cause may be that the children of richer families both tended to spend less time with their parents and reported feeling more emotionally isolated from their parents than did the children of more impoverished parents.[127] It's a result that should give any parent reason to pause and think. While money can buy our kids fabulous toys, a big garden to play in, and a great education, it can't guarantee them our time and attention.

I'm not claiming that I have easy answers. All I'm saying is that high attainment in any one area of our lives may often have consequences for other areas; we therefore need to be more aware of what we want and the trade-offs we're willing to make.

I pressed some of my clients to share with me their thoughts on having holistic, balanced visions. One of them replied in an email by saying: 'Of course when I stop to think about it, I know that my relationships are more important to me than how much I earn, the size of my bonus, the awards the team wins, and what my peers and competitors think of me and my work. Yet if you look at the last few years of my life or possibly all my career, outside observers would be hard pressed to say that I put as much effort into my relationships as I have into my work.'

Another client said: 'Looking back at my twenties and thirties, I did have the mentality that he who dies with the most toys wins. I still do to an extent. When I think about it, I can of course clearly see that money is only a means to an end. However, I am very driven by nature and must continue to remind myself that my career enables me to have a life rather than the other way around.'

Visioning is about formulating a balanced vision, considering the different facets, the multiple components that make up a thriving life. In business, any good manager knows the saying: 'What gets measured gets done.' So what are your measures of success?

BECOME YOUR BEST: Creating a balanced vision

Time to take an honest look at how you run your life – or is it your life that runs you? Project yourself into the distant future. Imagine that everything has gone as well as it possibly could. You have succeeded at accomplishing all of your life goals. Now write about what your life is like.

Remember that the point of a balanced vision is to ensure that you give sufficient weight to the different facets of a life that will make you feel fulfilled and successful. Here are some thoughts as to categories or components that you may wish to integrate into your vision:

- **Your physical life.** Consider your physical health, fitness, diet, energy levels, sleep patterns, and well-being.

- **Your relationships.** Think about the extent to which you need a loving relationship and/or sex with a partner, spouse, or significant other. Consider also your relationships with your parents, any siblings or children, and your wider flesh-and-blood ties. Don't forget about the quantity and quality of your social relationships too.

- **Future career and work achievements.** What financial, business, or career ambitions would you like to realise? But remember that you are not your job. Your job is merely one aspect of your life.

- **Future legacy and social achievements.** How do you want to be remembered? Think about your greater purpose or the meaning to your life. Consider what you would like to leave your family, the wider community, or even the planet once you're gone.

- **The present.** Remember not to fall into the trap of Destination Fixation, of waiting for some event on the horizon before you can allow yourself to feel satisfied and happy. If your definition of success is purely of a far-flung future destination, you could have a miserable time reaching it. Exceptional people not only strive for a better future but enjoy the present too. They work hard because they enjoy it – not just because they think it will bring them more money, status, or responsibility. And what pleasurable hobbies or enjoyable activities do you need to ensure you don't burn out along the way?

- **Personal values**. Psychologists agree that fulfilled people think not only about ends but also means. So think about not only what you want to achieve but also how you will get there, what kind of person you crave to be every day. Who would you be if your opinion was the only one that mattered? And what does that mean for how you behave from day to day?

Please don't consider those six groupings a comprehensive or prescriptive list of the components that you must include in your balanced vision. Remember that this is *your* masterpiece, your personal definition of prosperity and a life well lived. So feel free to introduce further elements, define your own categories, and include in your vision whatever you feel is important.

Most people have an idea of what success is – in their heads. And it's true that hardly anyone writes this stuff down. But that's the whole point of this book. *Most* people don't write this down so they rush around, stumbling and fumbling towards success. Without that clear direction, they take two steps forwards and occasionally three steps back. Only the exceptional few take the time to concoct a balanced vision.

Experts have long recognised that we have limited working memory. We find it strenuous to hold too much in our heads. For example, multiplying 367 by 819 using our mental prowess alone is almost impossible for most of us but relatively simple when using pencil and paper. Juggling multiple concepts in our heads doesn't work very well. So researchers agree that we can perform complex cognitive tasks much more effectively when we use external representations such as words or diagrams.[128]

If you were launching a business and needed a loan from a bank, you wouldn't tap the side of your head and say you've got the business plan in your head and don't need to write it down. And neither do schoolteachers accept assignments that their students have merely thought about.

Putting pen to paper (or fingers on keyboard) will help you to crystallise your balanced vision. A notion of success that lives only in your head can waver and fluctuate; it can't help you to make useful trade-offs and prioritise your resources. You get the point: write your vision down.

Visioning in practice

Too many people charge around without a clear idea of what they're trying to achieve. They hurtle along, trying to win prizes that aren't worth winning. Without a balanced vision, we too could rush to get 'there' faster without truly grasping why we want to get there or what we'll do once we arrive.

Exceptional people hit the pause button. They reflect on what matters to them.

When I work with people who created a balanced vision and referred to it over the course of months and years, I have seen them make positive changes in their lives. Gradually, they work towards achieving their goals and realising their passions; in stages, they reduce the tasks and parts of their lives that don't fulfil or inspire them.

But Visioning doesn't stop at merely conceiving a balanced vision. If we write a vision but then shove it away, we miss the point of having one. Visioning is also about using that balanced vision as a tool, a way to keep us motivated. Put your balanced vision somewhere where you will see it, refer to it, and use it to remind yourself of what's important and what's not.

Researchers know that simply imagining a desired future doesn't help people to achieve it. In reviewing published research on the power of mental imagery, university psychologists Noelia Vasquez and Roger Buehler agree that imagining future events can help to increase our motivation. However, they warn that 'positive mental images are more beneficial when they focus on precisely how the individual will attain the desired outcome (process focus) rather than exclusively on the outcome itself (outcome focus)'.[129] In other words, look at your vision and think about the concrete steps you can take towards it. Don't just fantasise and hope for your desired future to arrive in some magical way; make actual plans for tomorrow and the next day to make it happen.

But a little dreaming can still be good. Some experts believe that the mere act of dreaming about the future and reflecting on images of a desired future may even have physiological effects on us. A research team at Case Western Reserve University in the US argue that the power of pondering a personal vision 'is not just emotional. It is physical in that it involves neuro-endocrine processes that allow the body to renew itself, while ameliorating the ravages caused by chronic stress.'[130]

A well-constructed, balanced vision should be motivating and make us want to spring into action – or at least put a smile on our face. It should feel truly exciting, stretching us and encouraging us, rather than being a mere collection of goals. But it is not an immutable picture of the future that should forever be set in stone. Our visions should change as our lives change too. You're a different (hopefully better) person than you were only a few years ago and you will continue to evolve over the coming months and years. So my final piece of advice is to review your balanced vision and tweak it to keep it challenging but achievable. Whether you do it twice a year or once every two years is up to you. Just return to it occasionally to ensure it is constantly both exciting and right for you.

When we have a balanced vision, we can be focused. We can be clear in our goals. We can decide what we want not only in the future but also today. Rather than waiting to achieve success only at some far-flung future date, we can *be* a success every day.

Making the most of every day

This book is about exceptional people and how they carve out lives that are not only financially rewarding but personally fulfilling too. Perhaps the biggest barrier stopping many people from getting started is that they feel they have to earn a certain amount of money first.

I often hear people say: 'I just need to be financially se-cure – *then* I'll do what I really want to do.' They want to wait until they can pay off the mortgage or put the kids through school, get that next big promotion or perhaps just one more after that. Do you feel that you need a certain level of financial security before you can get started with the rest of your life?

Well, you're not alone. But some people make the leap any-way.

I first met Jason Dunne about five years ago. He was the commissioning editor of the global phenomenon that is the 'For Dummies' range of books. The bumblebee black-and-yellow-coloured books include titles ranging from *Currency Trading for Dummies* to *Buddhism for Dummies*. He approached me to write a book helping job hunters to succeed at interviews, and I eventually wrote *Answering Tough Interview Questions for Dummies*.

He was then promoted to become the publisher of the 'For Dummies' brand, in charge of a team that generated millions of pounds every year. But something didn't feel right.

'I did a couple of books that sold hundreds of thousands of copies and I was part of a team that put together a book that sold three million units. I'd been trying to get a hit that big my whole career. And when it came, I realised that it clocks up more numbers on a spreadsheet somewhere but it didn't mean that much to me. Or I realised that I wouldn't be sustained by it,' he tells me.

'That really galvanised me. The thing I'd been searching for didn't quite do it. I felt I wasn't learning anything new. I was going through the motions and even if I repeated that success, it wouldn't ring my bell.'

So he quit. He walked away from his six-figure salary, generous pension plan, and financial security. He turned his back on a job he was good at and a team he had hand-picked himself. Why?

Dunne has a vision not only of the life he wants to lead, but also the ways in which he believes technology is affecting the once-staid world of publishing. He foresees the traditional world of book publishing being turned on its head in the same way that the music business has changed beyond all recognition within the space of just a few years. The walls that divide television, publishing, and entertainment are crumbling – and Dunne wants in on the action.

He tells me about a couple of deals that he's discussing with major publishers to put their books on Apple's iPhone. The vision is to devise something that is more than a static book on an electronic device, to create interactive, immersive *experiences* that combine words, pictures, music, and even video on touch screen devices. I can't say too much as these things are commercially sensitive – I'd hate to give the game away and blow his chances.

Dunne is clear that he doesn't have the answers. He doesn't know for certain that he's on the right track. However, he feels as good as he has done in years.

'The way I feel is that all the problems that I face are my own doing. They are not problems that have been dumped on me. It makes all the difference in terms of my energy. I feel really alive actually, really alive,' he laughs.

'There's a fantastic quote, I think it was Thomas Huxley who said: "It is far better for a man to go wrong in freedom than to go right in chains." And although my employer was a good place to work and I had a nice team, I was basically working for somebody else's interests and I felt like I was in chains. I'd rather screw it all up on a project on my own than have my fate handed to me on a plate.'

Of course, Dunne isn't the only one to foresee the bound book go the way of the dinosaurs. The point, though, is that he's acting on it. Rather than sitting on the sidelines as an observer to the turmoil, he is throwing himself into the maelstrom.

Whether he's on target about the future of publishing is almost immaterial to him. He's almost nonchalant on the matter. What's apparent is that he is alive, passionate, invigorated. He loves his work again and is bubbling with excitement to be doing it.

'If you took me forward thirty years to show me that my venture didn't work, I wouldn't care. I'd be pleased that I gave it a go,' he concludes.

Can you say the same for your life?

Onwards and upwards

Visioning is a knack for creating a clear picture of what we want to achieve not only in our careers but in our whole lives. If you wish to learn from the best, here is how to get started:

- Most people don't have a vision, let alone a balanced vision of what they want to achieve and who they want to be. Be sure to invest time in considering what you want from your life to ensure you can be both successful and fulfilled.

- Don't underestimate the power of your imagination. Research shows that entrepreneurs who have visions of what they want to achieve end up with quantifiably more successful businesses. And even laboratory volunteers who are asked to imagine success on a test tend to perform better than those who don't.

- Avoid the trap of Destination Fixation, making your vision purely about what you want to achieve in the future. And consider not only what you want to *have* but also who you want to *be* – the kind of values and characteristics you wish to exemplify.

- Write your balanced vision down. Having a vision in your head is not quite the same as working out what you want in sufficient depth to feel comfortable committing it to a more permanent form.

- Remember that Visioning isn't just about creating a balanced vision but also using it as a compass, a decision-making tool to keep your life on track. Refer to it often. Steer clear of unsuitable situations or even people and seek out only opportunities that are consistent with your vision.

CONCLUSION

ONWARDS, UPWARDS AND OVER TO YOU

'An ounce of action is worth a ton of theory.'

Friedrich Engels

EXCEPTIONAL PEOPLE STAND OUT from the crowd. They're not necessarily more intelligent or gifted; they don't come from either better or worse backgrounds or benefit from extraordinary educations. In chronicling their journeys, I've only told fragments of their stories; in reality they all possess multiple capabilities. But I hope that the snippets I've shared manage to illustrate the capabilities – the skills and behaviours – that we may all be able to learn from.

As a psychologist, I work mainly with managers and entrepreneurs. I'm privileged to work with many talented, highly motivated people. I get paid by organisations to investigate (and then hopefully replicate for them) the factors that help some people to have stratospheric careers. And I have spent many thousands of hours both coaching people one-on-one as well as running large seminars on what it takes to succeed.

One of the biggest differences I see between high achievers and their less successful counterparts is that the exceptional ones are out there doing things. They take action. They take notes. They make plans. They initiate conversations and meetings and take steps every day to edge them closer towards their goals and visions. They consciously commit to self-improvement and make it a priority. Rather than just talking about what they *could* or *might* do, they get on with it.

I've run many training workshops and leadership development programmes over the years. So I know that not everyone takes the theories and principles that I teach and puts them into practice. More than a few people get bogged down in other tasks and forget or can't seem to find the time.

The same will probably be true for this book. I suspect that some readers will get to the end of this book and think, 'Yes, I knew that,' or 'That makes sense – I understand the principles.'

But understanding the principles isn't the same as actually deploying them.

Reading a book about tennis may give you ideas on how to improve your technique, but only hitting balls on a court will make you a better player. Understanding how Mozart constructed his piano concertos may expand your musical insight, but only playing the piano will make you a better pianist. Equally, reading about how someone lost weight may be inspiring; however, it's actually getting out and burning calories that will deliver the results.

The same goes for being more effective, productive, and fulfilled in our lives. None of the principles in this book are complicated. Yet understanding the principles alone won't help you to thrive; it's only through incorporating the techniques into your life every day that you will be able to learn, grow, and succeed. In contrast to traditional disclaimers, please *do* try these at home.

Get started

I hope I've inspired you to take action. Get Visioning. Incorporate just one or two new techniques into your repertoire. Share your thoughts on the book with a friend to keep the ideas at the forefront of your mind. Set aside even 15 minutes every day to do something differently. That should be easy, right? And you may find that small actions create their own momentum.

Flick back through the book and find the handful of exercises, techniques, or activities that resonate most strongly with you. Rather than trying to do everything at once, pick the ones that perhaps address the biggest gaps. Or maybe do the ones that sound like fun. Just do *something*.

If you are one of the few to draft a balanced vision and make plans for how to apply these capabilities every day, you will be in the minority, an exception. You will be in an even smaller minority if you review your progress from day to day and apply the principles within this book for at least 90 days. But then this book is about the small changes that allow the minority of absurdly successful people that we call high achievers to break free from the crowd. So being in a minority is definitely a plus.

Do send me an email to let me know how you get on. You can reach me at: rob@robyeung.com. I always enjoy hearing from readers, especially if you'd like to share your experiences, lessons, and tales of triumph. And do get in touch if you'd like me to work with your organisation too. I look forward to hearing about your successes.

Dr Rob Yeung

www.robyeung.com
www.talentspace.co.uk

Notes

1 Flanagan, J. C. (1947). 'The Aviation Psychology Program in the Army Air Forces'. *AAF Aviation Psychology Program Research Report No. 1*. Washington: US Government Printing Office.

2 Flanagan, J. C. (1954). 'The Critical Incident Technique'. *Psychological Bulletin*, 51, 327–358.

3 Judge, T. A., & Cable, D. M. (2004). 'The Effect of Physical Height on Workplace Success and Income: Preliminary Test of a Theoretical Model'. *Journal of Applied Psychology*, 89, 428–441.

4 Kristensen, P., & Bjerkedal, T. (2007). 'Explaining the Relation Between Birth Order and Intelligence'. *Science*, 316, 1717.

5 Dubow, E. F., Boxer, P., & Huesmann, L. R. (2009). 'Long-term Effects of Parents' Education on Children's Educational and Occupational Success: Mediation by Family Interactions, Child Aggression, and Teenage Aspirations'. *Merrill-Palmer Quarterly*, 55, 224–249.

6 As you can imagine, higher-income parents have greater resources to invest in their children's health, education, and so on, so their children tend to do better in life. But it seems that the income of a child's biological parents plays a role even when children are reared by non-biological parents – hence the title of the paper talks about 'nature *and* nurture' rather than nature versus nurture. Björklund, A., Jäntti, M., & Solon, G. (2007). 'Nature and Nurture in the Intergenerational Transmission of Socioeconomic Status: Evidence from Swedish Children and Their Biological and Rearing Parents'. *B.E. Journal of Economic Analysis & Policy*, 7, Article 4.

7 For example, many self-help gurus suggest that we should practise reciting affirmations such as 'I am successful' or 'I am loved'. However, research by reputable psychologists tells us that such affirmations may in some cases actually cause people's moods to plummet rather than improve: Wood, J. V., Perunovic, W. Q. E., & Lee, J. W. (2009). 'Positive Self-Statements: Power for Some, Peril for Others'. *Psychological Science*, 20, 860–866.

8 Simons, D. J., & Chabris, C. F. (1999). 'Gorillas in Our Midst: Sustained Inattentional Blindness for Dynamic Events'. *Perception*, 28, 1059–1074.

9 Wiseman, R. (2004). *The Luck Factor*. London: Arrow Books.

10 This example is written up in Langer's fascinating book on the health benefits of being more deliberately open-minded rather than simply accepting conventional wisdom about health. Langer, E. J. (2009). *Counterclockwise: Mindful Health and the Power of Possibility*. New York: Ballantine Books.

11 For more examples of when overly specific goals have made people – both experimental subjects as well as managers in businesses such as Ford, Enron, and Sears – focus too narrowly to the detriment of their work, see: Ordóñez, L. D., Schweitzer, M. E., Galinsky, A. D., & Bazerman, M H. (2009). 'Goals Gone Wild: The Systematic Side Effects of Over-Prescribing Goal Setting'. *Academy of Management Perspectives*, February, 6–16.

12 In an influential paper on productivity within large organisations, Paul Adler and colleagues argue: 'Routinization enables organizations to exploit their accumulated knowledge, increasing efficiency. At the same time, routinization creates a risk: when organizations are guided by old knowledge, they do not create new knowledge.' Adler, P. S., Benner, M., Brunner, D. J., MacDuffie, J. P., Osono, E., Staats, B. R., Takeuchi, H., Tushman, M. L., & Winter, S. G. (2009). 'Perspectives on the Productivity Dilemma'. *Journal of Operations Management*, 27, 99–113.

13 Sternberg, R. J. (2006). 'The Nature of Creativity'. *Creativity Research Journal*, 18, 87–98.

14 Chirumbolo, A., Livi, S., Mannetti, L., Pierro, A., & Kruglanski, A. W. (2004). 'Effects of Need for Closure on Creativity in Small Group Interactions'. *Journal of Personality*, 18, 265–278.

15 Researchers Wesley Cohen at Carnegie Mellon University and Daniel Levinthal at University of Pennsylvania argue that: 'a diverse background [of knowledge] provides a more robust basis for learning because it increases the prospect that incoming information will relate to what is already known. In addition to strengthening assimilative powers, knowledge diversity also facilitates the innovative process by enabling the individual to make novel associations and linkages.' For the full article, see: Cohen, W. M., & Levinthal, D. A. (1990). 'Absorptive Capacity: A New Perspective on Learning and Innovation'. *Administrative Science Quarterly*, 35, 128–152.

16 Boyatzis, R. E. (2006). 'Using Tipping Points of Emotional Intelligence and Cognitive Competencies to Predict Financial Performance of Leaders'. *Psicothema*, 18, 124–131.

17 For further reading on the need to strike a balance between depth and breadth of knowledge in creating a 'T-shaped' mind, see: Johansson, F. (2004). *The Medici Effect: Breakthrough Insights at the Intersection of Ideas, Concepts and Cultures*. Boston: Harvard Business School Press.

18 Duncker, K. (1945). 'On Problem Solving'. *Psychological Monographs*, 58 (5, Serial No. 270).

19 For an in-depth discussion of cultural gestures and their possible meanings, see: Chiu, C-y., & Hong, Y. (2006). 'Cultural Processes: Basic Principles'. In E. T. Higgins, & A. E. Kruglanski (eds.). *Social Psychology: Handbook of Basic Principles* (pp. 785–806). New York: Guilford Press.

20 Maddux, W. W., & Galinsky, A. D. (2009). 'Cultural Borders and Mental Barriers: The Relationship Between Living Abroad and Creativity'. *Journal of Personality and Social Psychology*, 96, 1047–1061.

21 Leung, A. K.-Y., & Chiu, C.-y. (2010). Multicultural Experience, Idea Receptiveness, and Creativity. *Journal of Cross-Cultural Psychology*, 41, 1–19.

22 Osborn, A. F. (1957). *Applied Imagination*. New York: Scribner.

23 Paulus, P. B., & Dzindolet, M. T. (1993). 'Social Influence Processes in Group Brainstorming'. *Journal of Personality and Social Psychology*, 64, 575–586.

24 Diehl, M., & Stroebe, W. (1987). 'Productivity Loss in Brainstorming Groups: Toward the Solution of a Riddle'. *Journal of Personality and Social Psychology*, 53, 497–509. Mullen, B., Johnson, C., & Salas, E. (1991). 'Productivity Loss in Brainstorming Groups: A Meta-Analytic Integration'. *Basic and Applied Social Psychology*, 12, 3–23.

25 This list of six bullet points is based on both my own experience as well as advice from researchers such as Vicky Putnam and Paul Paulus: Putnam, V. L., & Paulus, P. B. (2009). 'Brainstorming, Brainstorming Rules and Decision Making'. *Journal of Creative Behaviour*, 43, 23–39.

26 For a comprehensive review of social loafing in all sorts of situations, see: Karau, S. J., & Williams, K. D. (1993). 'Social Loafing: A Meta-Analytic Review and Theoretical Integration'. *Journal of Personality and Social Psychology*, 65, 681–706.

27 VanGundy, A. B. (1984). 'Brainwriting for New Product Ideas: An Alternative to Brainstorming'. *Journal of Consumer Marketing*, 1, 67–74.

28 Heslin, P. A. (2009). 'Better than Brainstorming? Potential Contextual

Boundary Conditions to Brainwriting for Idea Generation in Organizations'. *Journal of Occupational and Organizational Psychology*, 82, 129–145.

29   One study compared the effects of brainstorming alone followed by working together as a group versus working in a group and then working alone. In the 'alone to group' condition, the number of unique ideas generated per person was 66.9 when working individually and 39.9 when working together. In contrast, in the 'group to alone' condition, the number of unique ideas per person was lower, at only 33.8 ideas when working together and 56.4 ideas when working individually. Baruah, J., & Paulus, P. B. (2008). 'Effects of Training on Idea Generation in Groups'. *Small Group Research*, 39, 523–541.

30   My set of instructions is adapted from: Paulus, P. B., & Yang, H.-C. (2000). 'Idea Generation in Groups: A Basis for Creativity in Organizations'. *Organizational Behavior and Human Decision Processes*, 82, 76–87.

31   These four rules are adapted from: Treffinger, D. J., Isaksen, S. G., Stead-Dorval, K. B. (2005). *Creative Problem Solving: An Introduction. Waco: Prufrock Press.*

32   Author Daniel Goleman brought to the attention of the world the term 'emotional intelligence' with his popular book: Goleman, D. (1995). *Emotional Intelligence: Why It Can Matter More Than IQ.* New York: Bantam. However, for an excellent review of the scientific research, I recommend the work of researchers John Mayer and Peter Salovey, for example: Mayer, J. D., Salovey, P., & Caruso, D. R. (2004). 'Emotional Intelligence: Theory, Findings, and Implications'. *Psychological Inquiry*, 15, 197–215.

33   For a review of the ongoing trend towards greater workplace diversity, see: van Knippenberg, D., & Schippers, M. C. (2007). 'Work Group Diversity'. *Annual Review of Psychology*, 58, 515–541.

34   For a review of theory of mind research, have a look at: Flavell, J. H. (2004). 'Theory-of-Mind Development: Restrospect and Prospect'. *Merrill-Palmer Quarterly*, 50, 274–290.

35   Keysar, B., Lin, S., & Barr, D. J. (2003). 'Limits on Theory of Mind Use in Adults'. *Cognition*, 89, 25–41.

36   Wu, S., & Keysar, B. (2007). 'The Effect of Culture on Perspective Taking'. *Psychological Science*, 18, 600–606.

37   Galinsky, A. D., Magee, J. C., Inesi, M. E., & Gruenfeld, D. H. (2006). 'Power and Perspectives Not Taken'. *Psychological Science*, 17, 1068–1074.

38   Galinsky, A. D., Maddux, W. W., Gilin, D., & White, J. B. (2008). 'Why It Pays to Get Inside the Head of Your Opponent'. *Psychological Science*, 19, 378–384.

39   Studies in the workplace also show that making a greater effort to take the perspectives of others is related to higher job performance: Parker, S. K., & Axtell, C. M. (2001). 'Seeing Another Viewpoint: Antecedents and Outcomes of Employee Perspective Taking'. *Academy of Management Journal*, 44, 1085–1100.

40   Weyant, J. M. (2007). 'Perspective Taking as a Means of Reducing Negative Stereotyping of Individuals Who Speak English as a Second Language'. *Journal of Applied Social Psychology*, 37, 703–716.

41   Researchers such as the University of Georgia's Michael Kernis define Authenticity as: 'the unobstructed operation of one's true, or core, self in one's daily enterprise'. Take a look at this review paper for further background: Kernis, M. H. (2003). 'Toward a Conceptualization of Optimal Self-Esteem'. *Psychological Inquiry*, 14, 1–26.

42   Bakker, A. B. (2008). 'The Work-Related Flow Inventory: Construction and Initial Validation of the WOLF'. *Journal of Vocational Behavior*, 72, 400–414.

43 Judge, T. A., Thoresen, C. J., Bono, J. E., & Patton, G. K. (2001). 'The Job Satisfaction–Job Performance Relationship: A Qualitative and Quantitative Review'. *Psychological Bulletin*, 127, 376–407.

44 Peterson, C., Park, N., & Seligman, M. E. P. (2005). 'Orientations to Happiness and Life Satisfaction: The Full Life versus the Empty Life'. *Journal of Happiness Studies*, 6, 25–41.

45 Abele, A. E., & Spurk, D. (2009). 'How Do Objective and Subjective Career Success Interrelate Over Time?' *Journal of Occupational and Organizational Psychology*, 82, 803–824.

46 Csikszentmihalyi, M., & LeFevre, J. (1989). 'Optimal experience in work and leisure'. *Journal of Personality and Social Psychology*, 56, 815–822.

47 Salanova, M., Bakker, A. B., & Llorens, S. (2006). 'Flow at Work: Evidence for an Upward Spiral of Personal and Organizational Resources'. *Journal of Happiness Studies*, 7, 1–22.

48 Gardner, H. (2006). *Multiple Intelligences: New Horizons*. New York: Basic Books. For an accessible review of how multiple intelligences have been integrated into the curricula of many schools, see: Armstrong, T. (2009). *Multiple Intelligences in the Classroom*. Alexandria: Association for Supervision and Curriculum Development.

49 Wrzesniewski, A., & Dutton, J. E. (2001). 'Crafting a Job: Revisioning Employees as Active Crafters of their Work'. *Academy of Management Review*, 26, 179–201.

50 Janssen, O., & van Yperen, N. W. (2004). 'Employees' Goal Orientations, the Quality of Leader-Member Exchange, and the Outcomes of Job Performance and Job Satisfaction'. *Academy of Management Journal*, 47, 368–384.

51 For an in-depth exploration as to the purpose of inner speech, see: Morin, A. (1993). 'Self-Talk and Self-Awareness: On the Nature of the Relation'. *Journal of Mind and Behavior*, 14, 223–234.

52 There are literally hundreds of studies spanning four decades looking at the influence that negative and positive thoughts (often called 'cognitions') have on our moods. Here is just one short but good example: Ingram, R. E., & Wisnicki, K. S. (1988). 'Assessment of Positive Automatic Cognition'. *Journal of Consulting and Clinical Psychology*, 56, 898–902.

53 Burger, J. M., & Caldwell, D. F. (2000). 'Personality, Social Activities, Job-Search Behavior and Interview Success: Distinguishing Between PANAS Trait Positive Affect and NEO Extraversion'. *Motivation and Emotion*, 24, 51–62.

54 Seligman, M. E. P., & Schulman, P. (1986). 'Explanatory Style as a Predictor of Productivity and Quitting among Life Insurance Sales Agents'. *Journal of Personality and Social Psychology*, 50, 832–838.

55 Bono, J. E., & Ilies, R. (2006). 'Charisma, Positive Emotions and Mood Contagion'. *Leadership Quarterly*, 17, 317–334.

56 Van Kleef, G. A., Homan, A. C., Beersma, B., Van Knippenberg, D., Van Knippenberg, B., & Damen, F. (2009). 'Searing Sentiment or Cold Calculation? The Effects of Leader Emotional Displays on Team Performance Depend on Follower Epistemic Motivation'. *Academy of Management Journal*, 52, 562–580.

57 Diener, E., Nickerson, C., Lucas, R. E., & Sandvik, E. (2002). 'Dispositional affect and job outcomes'. *Social Indicators Research*, 59, 229–259. For a review of the effects of happiness on career success, take a look at this review paper: Boehm, J. K., & Lyubomirsky, S. (2008). 'Does Happiness Promote Career Success?' *Journal of Career Assessment*, 16, 101–116.

58 Lyubomirsky, S., King, L., & Diener, E. (2005). 'The Benefits of Frequent Positive Affect: Does Happiness Lead to Success?' *Psychological Bulletin*, 131, 803–855.

59 For an excellent overview of the contributions that nature and nurture make to a whole range of psychological traits and conditions, you could do worse than to read the musings of the leading scientist Sir Michael Rutter: Rutter, M. (2002). 'Nature, Nurture, and Development: From Evangelism through Science toward Policy and Practice'. *Child Development*, 73, 1–21.

60 In an excellent review of the research evidence, Sonja Lyubomirsky demonstrates that while our happiness is at least partly governed by a genetically determined set point for happiness, we can all employ certain techniques and practices to boost how we feel: Lyubomirsky, S., Sheldon, K. M., & Schkade, D. (2005). 'Pursuing Happiness: The Architecture of Sustainable Change'. *Review of General Psychology*, 9, 111–131.

61 There are thousands of studies demonstrating the efficacy of cognitive and behavioural techniques for improving people's mood and managing anxiety. The benefits are so well established that the UK's National Health Service encourages doctors to prescribe cognitive behavioural therapy (CBT) as the main form of treatment when patients have psychological disorders. Here is one fairly recent review paper: Hollon, S. D., Stewart, M. O., & Strunk, D. (2006). 'Enduring Effects for Cognitive Behavior Therapy in the Treatment of Depression and Anxiety'. *Annual Review of Psychology*, 57, 285–315.

62 Beitel, M., Ferrer, E., & Cecero, J. J. (2005). 'Psychological Mindedness and Awareness of Self and Others'. *Journal of Clinical Psychology*, 61, 739–750.

63 Barnes, S., Brown, K. W., Krusemark, E., Campbell, W. K., & Rogge, R. D. (2007). 'The Role of Mindfulness in Romantic Relationship Satisfaction and Responses to Relationship Stress'. *Journal of Marital and Family Therapy*, 33, 482–500.

64 Shao, R., & Skarlicki, D. P. (2009). 'The Role of Mindfulness in Predicting Individual Performance'. *Canadian Journal of Behavioural Science*, 41, 195–201.

65 Carson, J. W., Carson, K. M., Gil, K. M., & Baucom, D. H. (2004). 'Mindfulness-based Relationship Enhancement'. *Behavior Therapy*, 35, 471–494.

66 For a review of the benefits of mindfulness, see: Brown, K. W., Ryan, R. M., & Creswell, J. D. (2007). 'Mindfulness: Theoretical Foundations and Evidence for its Salutary Effects'. *Psychological Inquiry*, 18, 211–237. One study found that mindfulness training was able to reduce stress in patients with cancer, proving the power of the technique: Speca, M., Carlson, L. E., Goodey, E., & Angen, E. A. (2000). 'A Randomized Wait-List Controlled Clinical Trial: The Effects of a Mindfulness Meditation-Based Stress Reduction Program on Mood and Symptoms of Stress in Cancer Outpatients'. *Psychosomatic Medicine*, 62, 613–622.

67 There are hundreds of studies demonstrating the effectiveness of thought-recording techniques. For a review, see: Bennett-Levy, J. (2003). 'Mechanisms of Change in Cognitive Therapy: The Case of Automatic Thought Records and Behavioural Experiments'. *Behavioural and Cognitive Psychotherapy*, 31, 261–277.

68 Borton, J. L. S., & Casey, E. C. (2006). 'Suppression of Negative Self-Referent Thoughts: A Field Study'. *Self and Identity*, 5, 230–246.

69 Lyubomirsky, S., Sousa, L., & Dickerhoof, R. (2006). 'The Costs and Benefits of Writing, Talking, and Thinking About Triumphs and Defeats'. *Journal of Personality and Social Psychology*, 90, 692–708.

70 Kross, E., & Ayduk, O. (2008). 'Facilitating Adaptive Emotional Analysis: Distinguishing Distanced-Analysis of Depressive Experiences from Immersed-Analysis and Distraction'. *Personality and Social Psychology Bulletin*, 34, 924–938.

71 Pennebaker, J. W., Mayne, T. J., & Francis, M. E. (1997). 'Linguistic Predictors of Adaptive Bereavement'. *Journal of Personality and Social Psychology*, 72, 863–871.

72 Mark Leary at Duke University found that telling people to write about a negative event from a compassionate point of view had more benefits than simply asking people to write about the event from a neutral point of view: Leary, M. R., Tate, E. B., Adams, C. E., Allen, A. B., & Hancock, J. (2007). 'Self-Compassion and Reactions to Unpleasant Self-Relevant Events: The Implications of Treating Oneself Kindly'. *Journal of Personality and Social Psychology*, 92, 887–904.

73 Laura King at the University of Missouri observed that participants who wrote about a personal trauma for just two minutes each day for two consecutive days reported health benefits as compared to control participants who spent a similar amount of time writing about a neutral topic: Burton, C. M., & King, L. A. (2007). 'Effects of (Very) Brief Writing on Health: The Two-Minute Miracle'. *British Journal of Health Psychology*, 13, 9–14.

74 Yeung, R. R., & Hemsley, D. R. (1997). 'Personality, Exercise and Psychological Well-Being: Static Relationships in the Community'. *Personality and Individual Differences*, 22, 47–53.

75 Blumenthal, J. A., Babyak, M. A., Moore, K. A., Craighead, W. E., Herman, S., Khatri, P., Waugh, R., Napolitano, M. A., Forman, L. M., Appelbaum, M., Doraiswamy, P. M., & Krishnan, K. R. (1999). 'Effects of Exercise Training on Older Patients with Major Depression'. *Archives of Internal Medicine*, 159, 2349–2356.

76 For a review of research on physical exercise as a form of treatment for clinical depression, see: Brosse, A. L., Sheets, E. S., Lett, H. S., & Blumenthal, J. A. (2002). 'Exercise and the Treatment of Clinical Depression in Adults: Recent Findings and Future Directions'. *Sports Medicine*, 32, 741–760.

77 Yeung, R. R. (1996). 'The Acute Effects of Exercise on Mood State'. *Journal of Psychosomatic Research*, 40, 123–141.

78 Yeung, R. R., & Hemsley, D. R. (1996). 'Effects of Personality and Acute Exercise on Mood States'. *Personality and Individual Differences*, 20, 545–550.

79 Robinson, J. P., & Martin, S. (2008). 'What Do Happy People Do?' *Social Indicators Research*, 89, 565–571.

80 Frey, B. S., Benesch, C., & Stutzer, A. (2007). 'Does Watching TV Make Us Happy?' *Journal of Economic Psychology*, 28, 283–313.

81 Forret, M. L., & Sullivan, S. E. (2002). 'A Balanced Scorecard Approach to Networking: A Guide to Successfully Navigating Career Changes'. *Organizational Dynamics*, 31, 245–258.

82 For an excellent review of the importance of Connecting for people in non-profit organisations, see: King, N. K. (2004). 'Social Capital and Nonprofit Leaders'. *Nonprofit Management & Leadership*, 14, 471–486.

83 In a study of unemployed people looking for work, the University of Minnesota's Connie Wanberg and associates found that more than one in three people found their jobs through networking or through talking to friends, family, or previous colleagues: Wanberg, C. R., Kanfer, R., & Banas, J. T. (2000). 'Predictors and Outcomes of Networking Intensity Among Unemployed Job Seekers'. *Journal of Applied Psychology*, 85, 491–503.

84 Forret, M. L., & Dougherty, T. W. (2004). 'Networking Behaviors and Career Outcomes: Differences for Men and Women?' *Journal of Organizational Behavior*, 25, 419–437.

85 Wolff, H.-G., & Moser, K. (2009). 'Effects of Networking on Career Success: A Longitudinal Study'. *Journal of Applied Psychology*, 94, 196–206.

86 Forret, M. L., & Dougherty, T. W. (2004). 'Networking Behaviors and Career Outcomes: Differences for Men and Women?' *Journal of Organizational Behavior*, 25, 419–437.

87 Sørenson, J. (2007). 'Bureaucracy and Entrepreneurship: Workplace Effects on Entrepreneurial Entry'. *Administrative Science Quarterly*, 52, 387–412.

88 Christakis, N. A., & Fowler, J. H. (2007). 'The Spread of Obesity in a Large Social Network Over 32 Years'. *New England Journal of Medicine*, 357, 370–379.

89 Patacchini, E., & Zenou, Y. (2008). 'The Strength of Weak Ties in Crime'. *European Economic Review*, 52, 209–236.

90 Granovetter, M. S. (1973). 'The Strength of Weak Ties'. *American Journal of Sociology*, 78, 1360–1380.

91 Levin, D. Z., & Cross, R. (2004). 'The Strength of Weak Ties You Can Trust: The Mediating Role of Trust in Effective Knowledge Transfer'. *Management Science*, 50, 1477–1490.

92 Wright Brown, D., & Konrad, A. M. (2001). 'Granovetter Was Right: The Importance of Weak Ties to a Contemporary Job Search'. *Group & Organization Management*, 26, 434–462.

93 There are many studies demonstrating the protective effects of social networks on health, but here is just one good example: Vogt, T. M., Mullooly, J. P., Ernst, D., Pope, C. R., & Hollis, J. F. (1992). 'Social Networks as Predictors of Ischemic Heart Disease, Cancer, Stroke and Hypertension'. *Journal of Clinical Epidemiology*, 45, 659–666.

94 House, J. S., Landis, K. R., & Umberson, D. (1988). 'Social Relationships and Health'. *Science*, 241, 540–545.

95 Cohen, S., Doyle, W. J., Turner, R., Alper, C. M., & Skoner, D. P. (2003). 'Sociability and Susceptibility to the Common Cold'. *Psychological Science*, 14, 389–395.

96 Gilovich, T., & Medvec, V. H. (1995). 'The Experience of Regret: What, When, and Why'. *Psychological Review*, 102, 379–395.

97 Gilovich, T., Medvec, V. H., & Kahneman, D. (1998). 'Varieties of Regret: A Debate and Partial Resolution'. *Psychological Review*, 105, 602–605.

98 Keinan, A., & Kivetz, R. (2008). 'Remedying Hyperopia: The Effects of Self-Control Regret on Consumer Behavior'. *Journal of Marketing Research*, XLV, 676–689.

99 Gray, J. A. (1990). 'Brain Systems that Mediate both Emotion and Cognition'. *Cognition & Emotion*, 4, 269–288.

100 Elliot, A. J., & Sheldon, K. M. (1997). 'Avoidance Achievement Motivation: A Personal Goals Analysis'. *Journal of Personality and Social Psychology*, 73, 171–185.

101 Gable, S. L. (2006). 'Approach and Avoidance Social Motives and Goals'. *Journal of Personality*, 74, 175–222.

102 Locke, E. A., & Latham, G. P. (2002). 'Building a Practically Useful Theory of Goal Setting and Task Motivation'. *American Psychologist*, 57, 705–717.

103 Ariely, D., & Wertenbroch, K. (2002). 'Procrastination, Deadlines, and Performance: Self-Control by Precommitment'. *Psychological Science*, 13, 219–224.

104 Research tells us that the more we think about the steps needed to achieve a goal, the more likely we are to take successful action: Oettingen, G., Pak, H.-j., & Schnetter, K. (2001). 'Self-Regulation of Goal Setting: Turning Free Fantasies About the Future into Binding Goals'. *Journal of Personality and Social Psychology*, 80, 736–753.

105 For a comprehensive (although quite technical) review of research on self-efficacy, read: Bandura, A., & Locke, E. A. (2003). 'Negative Self-Efficacy and Goal Effects Revisited'. *Journal of Applied Psychology*, 88, 87–99.

106 For an excellent review of the difference between the fixed 'entity theory' and the dynamic 'malleable theory', see: Dweck, C. S., Chiu, C.-y., & Hong, Y.-y. (1995). 'Implicit Theories and Their Role in Judgments and Reactions: A World from Two Perspectives'. *Psychological Inquiry*, 6, 267–285.

107 Kray, L. J., & Haselhuhn, M. P. (2007). 'Implicit Negotiation Beliefs and Performance: Experimental and Longitudinal Evidence'. *Journal of Personality and Social Psychology*, 93, 49–64.

108 Sheri Levy's experiment was unpublished, but written up in: Levy, S. R., Plaks, J. E., Hong, Y.-y., Chiu, C.-y., & Dweck, C. S. (2001). 'Static Versus Dynamic Theories and the Perception of Groups: Different Routes to Different Destinations'. *Personality and Social Psychology Review*, 5, 156–168. And for a further review, see: Heslin, P. A., Latham, G. P., & VandeWalle, D. (2005). 'The Effect of Implicit Person Theory on Performance Appraisals'. *Journal of Applied Psychology*, 90, 842–856.

109 Blackwell, L. S., Trzesniewski, K. H., & Dweck, C. S. (2007). 'Implicit Theories of Intelligence Predict Achievement Across an Adolescent Transition: A Longitudinal Study and an Intervention'. *Child Development*, 78, 246–263.

110 Fraser, K. (2007). 'Conflicted Consumers'. *Harvard Business Review*, February, 35.

111 Haidt, J. (2007). 'The New Synthesis in Moral Psychology'. *Science*, 316, 998–1002.

112 *Our Common Future: Report of the World Commission on Environment and Development* (1987). World Commission on Environment and Development, Official Records of the General Assembly, Forty-second Session, Supplement No. 25 (A/42/427).

113 Winter, D. D. N. (2000). 'Some Big Ideas for Some Big Problems'. *American Psychologist*, 55, 516–522.

114 MacKay, D. J. C. (2009). *Sustainable Energy – Without the Hot Air*. Cambridge: UIT.

115 *The Business of Sustainability: Findings and Insights from the First Annual Business of Sustainability Survey and the Global Thought Leaders' Research Project* (2009). MIT Sloan Management Review Special Report.

116 Nidumolu, R., Prahalad, C. K., & Rangaswami, M. R. (2009). 'Why Sustainability Is Now the Key Driver of Innovation'. *Harvard Business Review*, September, 56–64.

117 Tanner, C., Wölfing Kast, S. (2003). 'Promoting Sustainable Consumption: Determinants of Green Purchases by Swiss Consumers'. *Psychology & Marketing*, 20, 883–902.

118 Baum, J. R., Locke, E. A., & Kirkpatrick, S. A. (1998). 'A Longitudinal Study of Vision and Vision Communication to Venture Growth in Entrepreneurial Firms'. *Journal of Applied Psychology*, 83, 43–54.

119 Baum, J. R., & Locke, E. A. (2004). 'The Relationship of Entrepreneurial Traits, Skill, and Motivation to Subsequent Venture Growth'. *Journal of Applied Psychology*, 89, 587–598.

120 Sherman, S. J., Skov, R. B., Hervitz, E. F., & Stock, C. B. (1981). 'The Effects of Explaining Hypothetical Future Events: From Possibility to Actuality and Beyond'. *Journal of Experimental Social Psychology*, 17, 142–158.

121 The 1987 poll by the *Chicago Tribune* is written up in: Myers, D. G., (1993). *The Pursuit of Happiness*. New York: Avon.

122 Diener, E., Horwitz, J., & Emmons, R. A. (1985). 'Happiness of the Very Wealthy'. *Social Indicators Research*, 16, 263–274.

123 For a review of this field of research, see: Diener, E., Ng, W., & Tov, W. (2008). 'Balance in Life and Declining Marginal Utility of Diverse Resources'. *Applied Research in Quality of Life*, 3, 277–291.

124 Aaron Ahuvia writes about his research in the following review paper: Ahuvia, A. (2008). 'If Money Doesn't Make Us Happy, Why Do We Act as If It Does?' *Journal of Economic Psychology*, 29, 491–507.

125 In reviewing studies on how people evaluate themselves, David Dunning and colleagues at Cornell University note that 'the appraisals that people endorse appear to be favorable to a logically impossible degree'. For example, 70 per cent of school students believe themselves to be above average in leadership with only 2 per cent rating themselves as below average. Amongst university lecturers, 94 per cent believe that they do above average work. Dunning, D., Meyerowitz, J. A., Holzberg, A. D. (1989). 'Ambiguity and Self-Evaluation: The Role of Idiosyncratic Trait Definitions in Self-Serving Assessments of Ability.' *Journal of Personality and Social Psychology*, 57, 1082–1090.

126 Researchers at the University of Michigan have found that the people who report being most satisfied with their lives not only work towards meaningful long-term goals but also make time for engaging and pleasurable activities in the present: Peterson, C., Park, N., & Seligman, M. E. P. (2005). 'Orientations to Happiness and Life Satisfaction: The Full Life Versus the Empty Life.' *Journal of Happiness Studies*, 6, 25–41.

127 Luthar, S. S., & Latendresse, S. J. (2005). 'Children of the Affluent: Challenges to Well-Being.' *Current Directions in Psychological Science*, 14, 49–53.

128 Zhang, J., & Wang, H. (2009). 'An Exploration of the Relations between External Representations and Working Memory'. *PLoS ONE*, 4, e6513.

129 Vasquez, N. A., & Buehler, R. (2007). 'Seeing Future Success: Does Imagery Perspective Influence Achievement Motivation?' *Personality and Social Psychology Bulletin*, 33, 1392–1405.

130 Boyatzis, R. E., & Akrivou, K. (2006). 'The Ideal Self as the Driver of Intentional Change.' *Journal of Management Development*, 25, 624–642.

Index

A

extracts reading groups
competitions books new
discounts extracts
competitions extracts
books new discounts
new books events reading groups
interviews events books
new reading groups
interviews events new
events extracts extracts events books
discounts interviews new books extracts
new books events events new books interviews
events new interviews new books extracts
discounts extracts discounts
www.panmacmillan.com
extracts events reading groups
competitions books extracts new books